Are We Becoming Two Societies?

Income Polarization and the Myth of the Declining Middle Class in Canada

Charles M. Beach
and
George A. Slotsve

with comments by
Alan Harrison
and
Chris Sarlo

The Social
Policy Challenge 12

John Richards
and
William G. Watson,
Series Co-Editors

C.D. Howe Institute

C.D. Howe Institute publications are available from:
Renouf Publishing Company Limited, 1294 Algoma Road,
Ottawa, Ontario K1B 3W8; phone (613) 741-4333; fax (613) 741-5439

and from Renouf's stores at:
71½ Sparks Street, Ottawa (613) 238-8985
12 Adelaide Street West, Toronto (416) 363-3171

For trade book orders, please contact:
McGraw-Hill Ryerson Limited, 300 Water Street,
Whitby, Ontario L1N 9B6; phone (416) 430-5050

Institute publications are also available in microform from:
Micromedia Limited, 165 Hôtel de Ville, Place du Portage, Phase II,
Hull, Quebec J8X 3X2

This book is printed on recycled, acid-free paper.

Canadian Cataloguing in Publication Data

Beach, Charles M.
    Are we becoming two societies?

(The social policy challenge ; 12)
Includes bibliographical references.
ISBN 0-88806-343-1

1. Income distribution – Canada. 2. Middle
class – Canada – Economic conditions. I. Slotsve,
George A. II. C.D. Howe Institute. III. Title.
IV. Series.

HC120.I5B42 1996   339.2′2′0971   C96-930383-1

Cover design by Leroux Design Inc.
Printed in Canada by Kromar Printing Ltd.,
Winnipeg, Manitoba, March 1996.

Contents

Figures

Tables

Foreword

This volume is the twelfth in the C.D. Howe Institute's "The Social Policy Challenge," one of the most ambitious series of publications in its history. The 15 studies in the series range from workfare to pensions, from unemployment insurance (UI) to workers' compensation, from housing to aboriginal concerns.

The publication of this series is a daunting task not just for its scope, but also for the urgency and importance of the issues it addresses. Canada needs to modernize its basic social programs — programs that were conceived in an era of economic growth and expanding benefits for the recipients of ever-multiplying public services.

Like many other Canadians, I believe the time is right for a wholesale re-examination of this country's social policies. There are several reasons why.

First, Canada's fiscal situation remains perilous: despite rapid economic growth, the combined borrowing of Ottawa and the provinces still amounts to about $60 billion annually. Such high deficits mean that Canada's debt will continue to grow more quickly than its economic output, which in turn means the ratio of debt to gross domestic product (GDP) will keep on rising, as it has without exception since 1977. With still higher debt-to-GDP ratios, interest payments will consume an even greater share of public budgets, and the country's finance ministers will remain at the mercy of swings in interest rates.* We do not necessarily have to reduce the debt ratio — though our children would appreciate it if we did — but we must stop it from growing.

---

* See Thomas E. Kierans and William B.P. Robson et al., *The Courage to Act: Fixing Canada's Budget and Social Policy Deficits*, C.D. Howe Institute Commentary 64 (Toronto: C.D. Howe Institute, October 1994).

Expenditures on social programs are such an important part of public spending that a re-evaluation of how they work simply must be part of the solution.

Second, Canada is at a crossroads. The phrase is, of course, a rhetorician's reflex. Hardly a year goes by without someone's publishing a volume with that title. And to some extent the cliché is always appropriate: modern democracies make policy decisions almost daily, so they are continually at a crossroads. Still, 1995 will likely see changes to federal-provincial transfers — and possibly the taxing powers of the two levels of government as well.

Everything is on the table for discussion. No doubt, a consensus is developing that Canada has hit the ceiling when it comes to taxes. Even Canadians of the middle-of-the-road variety are no longer willing to finance the apparently unending expansion of the welfare state into more and more marginal activities.

Third, there is increasing concern that many of the programs Canadian governments have put in place over the years may not be good for the people they are supposed to help. Within the academic community, it is now respectable to speak of "transfer dependency," a concept for which economist Thomas Courchene was widely criticized when he introduced it into the Canadian debate in the 1970s. Politicians and commentators across the ideological spectrum now agree that policies that were introduced for very good short-term reasons have created harmful long-term incentives. For example, many Canadians have changed their lifestyles to conform to the rules of the UI and welfare systems. As the growth of Ontario's welfare caseload illustrates, transfer dependency may no longer be a problem exclusive to the Atlantic region.

Canadians and their governments thus are likely to be preoccupied with social policy over the next few years. It is with this in mind that the C.D. Howe Institute decided to undertake this in-depth examination of social programs. In choosing the co-editors of the series — John Richards, Associate Professor of Business Administration at Simon Fraser University, and William Watson, Associate Professor of Economics, McGill University

— I sought to bring a balance of views to the Institute's work. John Richards was a member of Allan Blakeney's New Democratic government in Saskatchewan in the early 1970s. William Watson terms himself "a member of that beleaguered cultural minority, the Canadian right." Although both are experts in the field of economics, neither had previously concentrated his formidable energies in the social policy area, and I felt they would bring a fresh view to some of the same old policy conundrums.

Readers will note that each volume will contain differing, at times opposing, views as to whether a particular social program works as intended, needs fixing, or should be left alone. If the conclusion is that a program does need modernizing, the authors will recommend necessary reforms and ways to bring them about.

The C.D. Howe Institute's aim in presenting this series is to raise the level of public debate on issues of national interest by presenting diverse points of view — whether or not it agrees with them — in publications that are well researched and well grounded. The Institute hopes that, in so doing, it will give Canadians much to think about, including the information they require to exercise their responsibilities as citizens.

This volume was copy edited by Leah Johnson and Riça Night, and prepared for publication by Barry A. Norris. The analysis and opinions presented in the study are the responsibility of the authors and do not necessarily reflect the views of the Institute's members or Board of Directors.

Thomas E. Kierans
President and
Chief Executive Officer

Acknowledgments

The authors thank the C.D. Howe Institute and Professor Bill Watson for whetting our interest in and sponsoring the following study on the topic of polarization and the middle class in Canada. We also extend special thanks to Glenn Griffis for helpful conversations; to Brian Lewis and Colin McCormick for excellent assistance on the project; to Riça Night for super editorial work on the manuscript; and to David Brown, John Richards, and Bill Watson for extensive detailed remarks on an earlier draft. We retain full responsibility for all limitations that may remain.

The Study in Brief

Inequality is the issue of the hour. Canadians who live in large cities are regularly confronted by beggars, desperate souls seeking cash, though because "beggars" has such a Third-World ring we prefer to call them "homeless." The news media regularly report increases in the poverty rate. Of course, they also report, or at least did in early 1996, both record earnings by corporations and record-breaking increases in stock prices.[1] That the rich are getting richer and the poor at best breaking even is now almost a truism in Canada. It is also widely agreed that, as elsewhere in the industrialized world, with incomes becoming steadily more polarized, the middle class is gradually vanishing. Whether this all owes more to deregulation, corporate downsizing, government deficit reduction, free trade, or "globalization" is still hotly debated, but with the income distribution spreading out, with its extremes growing, with the gulf between "haves" and "have-nots" widening, the idea is now commonplace that, to all intents and purposes, we are becoming two societies.

Except that we are not. This twelfth volume in the C.D. Howe Institute's "The Social Policy Challenge" series, written by economists Charles Beach, from Queen's University, Kingston, Ontario, and George Slotsve, from Vanderbilt University, Nashville, Tennessee, takes a hard look at the statistics of Canadian income distributions and finds that, in fact, there has been much less polarization of incomes than public discussion of the issue would suggest. And what there has been is all but completely explained by cyclical factors: when the unemployment rate rises, so does inequality, but when the unemployment rate falls, inequality falls

---

1 They are right about the stock market, but wrong about corporate profits, which are at record levels only in nominal dollar terms. In real dollars and as a share of gross domestic product, they are nowhere near record highs.

too. The data reveal hardly any long-run trend toward income polarization, and for some categories of income earners, notably women, polarization has actually fallen. The popular impression may be that, every day, in every way, the world is getting worse and worse. But the numbers do not bear that out. Income inequality goes through its ups and downs, but it is not steadily rising. As the authors themselves say in their summing up:

> To the question posed in the title of this study — Are We Becoming Two Societies? — the answer suggested by the evidence is "no." The 1980s saw much more marked changes in polarization rates than did the 1970s. But the changes were concentrated primarily in two periods, 1974–85 and 1989–92. They were also heavily affected by standard business cycle fluctuations, particularly by the two severe recessions at opposite ends of the decade. The 1980s were not so much a new era of polarization in Canada as an era of slower economic growth, higher taxes, and two severe recessions that had marked distributional effects. (p. 126.)

Polarization of Incomes

The Beach and Slotsve study contains a large number of results. This "Study in Brief" tries to summarize its more important and perhaps unexpected findings, beginning with the polarization of incomes:

- There was almost no increase in the polarization of family incomes between 1972 and 1992 (see Table 12). Together, people whose incomes were more than 175 percent or less than 25 percent of the median increased from 18.0 percent of the population to 19.2 percent, a rise of only 2.5 percentage points over 20 years. And even this rather modest increase in polarization was not polarization of the traditional sort, which involves both ends of the distribution getting bigger.

Rather, those families making less than 25 percent of the median income fell from 5.3 percent of the population to 3.9 percent, which presumably should be regarded as good news, while those making more than 175 percent of the median income increased from 12.7 percent of the population to 15.3 percent.[2]

- Polarization among female income recipients actually *fell* — more or less steadily — over the past two decades (see Table 8). Thus, the proportion of women making either below 25 percent or above 175 percent of the female median income declined from 44.1 percent in 1972 to 38.7 percent in 1992. In this case, both extremes of the distribution became smaller. Those making less than 25 percent of the median fell from 14.5 percent to 11.9 percent of female earners, while those making more than 175 percent of the median fell from 29.6 percent to 26.8 percent. Beach and Slotsve report that, when they "control for cyclical factors...the estimated decline [in female polarization rates] is half a percentage point per year, or 10.2 percentage points over the full period" (p. 72).

- Male income recipients did experience first an increase (from 1972 to 1983), then a reduction (from 1983 to 1989), then, finally, another increase in polarization (from 1989 to 1992; see Table 7), but these changes are completely explained by (presumably cyclical) changes in unemployment. Men making incomes either below 25 percent or above 175 percent of the median income increased from 28.4 percent to 32.6 percent of male income recipients. Again, this was the combined

---

2 The median income is found by ranking everybody according to their income and then finding out what the person halfway down the line makes. The tails of a distribution can be cut off at any point, of course, and looking at people below 25 percent and above 175 percent of the median is just one way of doing it. Beach and Slotsve also compare people making less than half the median income with those making 150 percent and 200 percent of the median. Only the 25/175 figures are quoted here, mainly to assure that this introduction remains just a summary.

effect of a *fall* in the numbers of men making less than 25 percent of the median — from 13.5 percent of the population to 11.5 percent — and an increase in the proportion making more than 175 percent of the median from 14.9 percent to 21.1 percent. As the authors note, however, "when we control for cyclical factors, polarization rates for men are not estimated to change significantly over the 1972–92 period" (p. 72.)

In sum, the degree of polarization of family incomes barely budged over the 20 years; the polarization of women's incomes declined; and the polarization of men's incomes, while rising from start to end, was mainly determined by the business cycle. Moreover, through much of the 1980s — certainly through the boom years of that decade — most measures of polarization were declining, which is not the impression most people have of the "decade of greed."

Polarization in Earnings

The results just reported concern the polarization of *income*. Income includes government transfers, pensions, and investment income. For most people, however, the most important component of income is *earnings* — wages, salaries, and net self-employment income. Beach and Slotsve find that, in general, the polarization of earnings has increased more than the polarization of income. Even here, however, changes have not been as dramatic as might have been expected:

- Between 1971 and 1992, males who earned less than 25 percent or more than 175 percent of median male earnings increased from 29.4 percent to 39.1 percent of all male earners, which does indicate increasing polarization (see Table 5). This change was made up of both an increase in the bottom group, from 15.5 to 18.1 percent of earners, and a larger increase in the top group, from 13.9 to 21.0 percent of earners. Thus, the bottom group grew by 2.6 percentage points and the top group by 7.1 percentage points. The overall increase in polarization, however, was not steady. The combined share of the two groups changed little through the 1970s, rose sharply during the recession of the early 1980s, declined gradually between 1984 and 1989, and then rose again as a result of the post–1989 recession. As was also true for male incomes, controlling for cyclical factors reveals very little long-run increase in the polarization of male earnings — an increase of only one-eighth of one percent per year (Table A-2). That earnings inequality is strongly influenced by the business cycle — rising in bad times and falling in good — is, in fact, well known in the literature. In Beach and Slotsve's data set, the precise dimensions of the relationship are that an increase of one percentage point in the unemployment rate raises male earnings polarization by 1.35 percentage points (Table A-2). It is not surprising, therefore, that, in their conclusions, the authors suggest public policy focus on measures to increase employment.

- As was also true for female incomes, the polarization of female earnings fell between 1971 and 1992 (see Table 6). There is, in addition, a clear cyclical component in female polarization. Once cyclical changes in unemployment were controlled for, female polarization declined at a rate of about a quarter of a percentage point per year. Although unemployment does not have quite as dramatic an effect on the polarization of female earnings as male earnings, polarization does rise by almost nine-tenths of a percentage point for every one percentage point increase in the national unemployment rate (Table A-2). Despite the long-run decline in female polarization rates, they remain at least five points greater than the corresponding rates for males, reflecting the more diverse labor force habits of females.

The Middle Class Is Not Shrinking

People who are not at either end of the income distribution must be in the middle — and somewhere in the middle the (in fact, difficult-to-define) "middle class" is likely to be found. To see what has been happening to this class, Beach and Slotsve calculate how many people have been making incomes bracketed by the median income. They look at people making plus or minus 15 percent of the median, 25 percent, 50 percent, and so on. Not surprisingly, their results for what has happened in the middle are just the mirror image of what has happened outside the middle.

The female middle class has actually grown slightly. Women making more than 25 percent but less than 175 percent of the median income were 55.9 percent of all female income earners in 1972, 58.2 percent in 1982, and 61.4 percent in 1992 (Table 10). In fact, "women's middle-class population shares all show a distinct upward trend...over the 1972–92 period, with no significant cyclical pattern" (p. 80). The male middle class, on the other hand, has shrunk slightly, with those making between 25 percent and 175 percent of the median male income falling from 71.6 percent of the population in 1972 to 67.6 percent in 1982 to 67.4 percent in 1992 (Table 11). Again, however, a strong cyclical pattern is evident in the movement of this male-middle-class ratio. The authors' statistical tests show that once it is taken into account there is no significant trend in the middle-class share for men; once again it is cyclical factors that drive the results. A decrease in the unemployment rate by one percentage point and a tightening up of the labor market are estimated to increase the middle-class share for men by 0.77 of a percentage point.

The results for family incomes are consistent with those for men and women separately: "All measures but the widest peak in 1974 and...trough during the 1982–85 period associated with the severe recession at the beginning of the 1980s" (p. 90). In other words, the middle class shrank between the mid-1970s and mid-1980s but then generally grew following the early 1980s' recession, only to decline at least somewhat once the recession that began in 1989 hit. Beach and Slotsve find that "[t]he most marked declines in the size of the middle class...occurred over the decade 1974–85" (pp. 94–95), which is hardly the common impression, and they conclude "we found no statistically significant trend over the 1972–92 period as a whole. That is, the size of the middle class does not seem to have decreased over the past two decades once cyclical factors are taken into account" (p. 92).

Middle-Class Incomes Are Stagnant

Although Beach and Slotsve's results on polarization tend to be reassuring, indicating that, despite newspaper wisdom, there has been no long-run trend toward greater polarization of incomes in Canadian society, their findings regarding the absolute growth of income are more disturbing.

While the middle class has been holding its own in terms of population share, it has been earning a declining share of overall income. This actually is not true for female income earners: by all measures of the female middle class, middle-income earners have increased their share of total female income (Table 10). But it is true for men and for families. For instance, as already noted, between 1972 and 1992 men making between 25 percent and 175 percent of the median income fell from 71.6 percent of the population to 67.4 percent, a drop of 4.2 percentage points (Table 11). At the same time, their share of total male earned income fell from 63.9 percent to 53.4 percent, a decline of 10.5 points, more than double, which indicates that, in relative terms at least, they are not doing as well as they used to. Although it may not be shrinking, the middle class is getting relatively poorer. In the same way, while families with incomes between 25 and 175 percent of the median income declined from 82.0 percent of families in 1972 to 80.8 in 1992, a decline of only 1.2 percentage points, their share of total family income fell from 71.1 percent to 66.9 percent, a decline of 4.2 percentage points (Table 14). These may not be large changes, but they do confirm that proportionately more income has been going to people at the extremes of the income distribution. For example, for males all of the increase has taken place at the top end. Those making less than 25 percent of the median income have seen their share of total income drop (from 1.62 percent of the total to 1.14 percent; see Table 7), while men making more than 175 percent of median male income accounted for only 34.5 percent of total male income in 1972 but fully 45.4 percent in 1992. Again, it is interesting that most of this increase had taken place by the early 1980s: through that decade, top income earners' share of total income actually declined, until turning up slightly with the onset of the post–1989 recession.

The pattern for families is similar, though much less dramatic: the income share of those making more than 175 percent of the median rose between 1972 and 1992 from 28.2 percent of the total to 32.6 percent (Table 12). The share of those making less than 25 percent of the median fell from 0.74 percent of the total to 0.53 percent. Again, there is a strong cyclical component to the movement of these income shares, and most of the change had taken place by the early 1980s, after which upper shares mainly declined, though they did turn up again after 1989.

Even more direct evidence that the middle class has experienced little income growth in recent years is provided by Beach and Slotsve's examination of what has happened to incomes in dollar terms. Women actually have not done badly: from 1971 to 1992 the average income of the middle 60 percent of female income recipients rose more or less steadily from about $9,500 a year to about $15,500 (in 1991 dollars; see Figure 12). The only times in which women's real incomes fell were during the 1981–82 recession, when they declined by roughly $400, and during the 1990–92 recession, when the decline was about half that. By contrast, the average real income of male income recipients went through a roller-coaster ride over these 21 years (see Figure 13). It started out at about $24,600, rose above $29,000 in the mid-1970s, fell back to below $26,000 in the mid-1980s, made it to about $27,500 in the 1980s' expansion, and fell back below

$26,000 in the early 1990s recession.[3] On the other hand, the differing fortunes of male and female income recipients combined to produce a growth path of family income that was not nearly so vertiginous. The average real income of the middle 60 percent of families was a little above $37,000 in 1971, rose to almost $48,000 in the early 1980s, dipped to just above $44,000 after the early 1980s' recession, reached $50,000 in the 1980s' expansion, and fell to below $48,000 in the post–1989 recession. Not exactly smooth sailing, but hardly as bumpy a ride as men experienced on their own.

While average family incomes grew by 24.4 percent between 1972 and 1991, they rose only 2.6 percent between 1980 and 1991 (note to Table 13). The choice of end years biases this comparison at least somewhat, since 1980 marked a relative peak for incomes, while 1991 was a trough year, but as the numbers quoted in the previous paragraph indicate, despite the impressive expansion from 1984 to 1989, the 1980s as a whole were not a banner decade for income growth.

Not all families did poorly in the 1980s, however. The real incomes of families headed by people who were 65 or older at the end of the decade were a quarter higher than those of families headed by people that age at the beginning of the decade. Families headed by people aged 45–54 were 9.5 percent better off than similar families at the beginning of the decade (and a third better off than such families had been in 1972). On the other hand, families headed by people aged 35–44 were barely better off in 1991 than similar families had been in 1980, and families headed by people aged less than 35 were decidedly worse off: to be precise, families headed by people aged 20–24 made 17.6 percent less in 1991 than similar families had made in 1980 (Table 13). Statistical analysis for the entire 1972–91 period reveals an upward trend in real incomes of about 1.3 percent per year but also a strong cyclical

---

3 The net effect of the differing fortunes of men and women is that "[t]he earnings gap between men and women clearly narrowed during the 1970–92 period, but the narrowing was due partly to falling men's earnings, not just to rising women's earnings" (p. 58).

effect: an increase of one percentage point in the unemployment rate caused a 1.5 percent reduction in average family income.

The Increasing Tax Burden

All the results reported so far have dealt with before-tax income. Although the data Beach and Slotsve use do not allow them to look at the influence of *all* taxes, they are able to take account of the effects of federal and provincial personal income taxes, which constitute about half the personal tax burden. Among other things, they conclude that:

> The tax burden rose from 13.3 percent of median family income in 1971 to a 1991 peak of 17.6 percent. Almost all of the 4.5 percentage point rise...occurred in the 1980s. The average rate of growth in median after-tax family income was 2.51 percent per year from 1971 to 1980 and 0.05 percent per year — basically no growth at all — from 1980 to 1992. (p. 98.)

The corresponding growth rates of pre-tax median income were 2.65 and 0.44 percent per year, respectively. Thus, taxation cut the growth of median income by 0.14 of a percentage point a year in the 1970s and by 0.39 of a percentage point a year in the 1980s. In percentage terms, the growth of median incomes was trimmed by 5.3 percent (= 0.14/2.65 x 100) in the 1970s but by 88.6 percent (= 0.39/0.44 x 100) in the 1980s. As the authors note, "after-tax incomes in 1992 were essentially where they were 15 years earlier, in 1976" (p. 100).

In 1989, the best year for incomes in the 1980s, the middle 60 percent of families earned an average of $50,068 in real (1991) dollars, the only time between 1972 and 1992 that this number exceeded $50,000. Out of this amount, the average family in this group took home $41,322. Yet, while the average family was making $2,512 more in gross income in 1989 than in 1980, it was taking home only $587 more. In effect, 76.6 percent of the difference in pre-tax income between the two years had been eaten up by taxes (calculated from Table A-7).

As before, the results for family income represent an amalgam of contrasting results for men and women. The average after-tax income of men declined more or less steadily from its peak in 1976, and in 1992 was only $201 higher than it had been in 1971 ($23,250). Women's average income, on the other hand, grew more or less steadily between 1971 and 1992, from a little over $10,000 a year (in 1991 dollars) to a little under $16,000 a year (Figure 18). As a result, women's average after-tax income increased from 44 percent of men's in 1971 to 66 percent in 1992 (calculated from Table A-9). Men's average personal income tax rate rose from 16.1 percent in 1971 to 20.9 percent in 1992, while women's rose from 12.0 percent to 15.8 percent over the same period.

In every year from 1971 to 1992 the income tax system was "progressive by quintiles" — that is, the lowest-earning fifth of taxpayers paid the lowest tax rates, the second-lowest the second-lowest rates, and so on (Table 16). In 1992, the bottom fifth of taxpayers faced an average tax rate of only 3.0 percent, while the top fifth paid 25.2 percent. For the 1971–92 period, tax rates increased by a quarter. No doubt it will surprise many people to learn that, from 1980 to 1992, tax rates increased most rapidly in the top quintile (by 29 percent), followed by the second quintile from the top (23 percent), the middle quintile (18 percent), the bottom quintile (11 percent), and, finally, the second quintile from the bottom (9 percent). In another essentially contrarian passage, Beach and Slotsve conclude that

> the income tax burden on the middle class increased *less* in the 1980s than did the average tax rate for all Canadian families. The reason for this is that the average tax rate for upper- and middle-upper-income families increased *markedly more* over the period, thereby pulling up the average tax burden across all families. While the middle-class tax burden did indeed increase substantially during the 1980s, it rose proportionally less than did the tax burden for the upper portions of the distribution. (p. 107; emphasis added.)

Beach and Slotsve's results on overall inequality will also surprise many people. Although market income — that is, income before taxes and transfers, such as income assistance, unemployment insurance, workers' compensation, the Canada and Quebec Pensions Plans, and the former family allowances — has become somewhat less equally distributed, other income aggregates have become more equally distributed. As the authors say:

> Between 1980 and 1992, inequality in market incomes rose by 14.3 percent..., but when [mainly government] transfers are added in, inequality in total income increased by only 5.3 percent. Transfers thus largely compensated for rising inequality in market incomes during the 1980s. The effect of income taxes has also been to reduce inequality quite substantially...*[T]he size of the reduction in inequality increased quite markedly in the 1980s as the upper-income groups saw their taxes rise relatively more.* (p. 104; emphasis added.)

In total, Beach and Slotsve argue, income tax changes "reduced income inequality...by about 40 to 50 percent of the corresponding inequality-reducing effect of government transfers" (p. 108). It is possible, of course, that changes in other taxes through the 1980s may have offset these effects. Still, public opinion seems to believe that the income tax system itself became skewed in the 1980s toward the interests of the rich. Such a conclusion is not warranted by Beach and Slotsve's data.

Objectively, Economic Insecurity Has Fallen

Although there has been no long-run trend toward income polarization and although middle-class income taxes may have risen less than taxes did at the upper end of the income distribution, the years since 1980 have hardly been good ones for middle-income earners. As Beach and Slotsve put it, "[m]edian family after-tax income essentially did not grow at all in the 1980s; in

1992, it was virtually the same as it had been 16 years earlier" (p. 107). These and other developments have given rise to a widely noted increase in economic insecurity. Beach and Slotsve's final statistical exercise tries to estimate the state of what might be called "objective economic insecurity." Whatever people may have felt about their economic chances, how much more likely was it that they would suffer a fall in their income? And if their income did suffer such a fall, how much further would it fall now than it would have in previous decades?

To examine the first type of insecurity — the possibility of experiencing a decline in economic status — Beach and Slotsve examine the relative sizes of different income groups. If everyone in a given income class is equally likely to fall from it, then the chance of actually moving down is equal to the relative size of the two income classes. To calculate this risk, the authors therefore compare the number of people making a middle-class income with the number making below a middle-class income. If there are lots of higher-income earners and not many lower-income earners, the chance of moving down may not be great, so insecurity should be low. If the proportion is reversed, however, both the chance of moving down and, therefore, insecurity should be greater.[4]

To examine the second aspect of insecurity — how far you fall if you do fall — it makes sense to look at the difference between the mean incomes of the two groups. If you fell from making the mean income of the higher-income group to making the mean income of the lower-income group, what percentage reduction in income would you suffer?[5]

---

4 In fact, the chance of slipping from one group to another probably is not random (that is, equally likely to happen to anyone in the group). Some people in a given income class probably are more at risk of falling out of it than are others. Unfortunately, available data do not allow us to know who faces precisely what risk.

5 Of course, it may be that no one ever moves from making exactly the mean income in a higher-income group to making exactly the mean income in a lower-income group, but in the absence of better data on intergroup mobility, this is probably the best that can be done.

Finally, by multiplying the two measures together — that is, the chance of falling times the extent of the fall — Beach and Slotsve obtain some idea of the sorts of economic losses people might reasonably expect to suffer. For instance, if your income fell by $12,000 if it did fall, but if there were only a 1-in-3 chance that it would fall, then your expected loss would be $4,000. Has that expected loss risen, fallen, or stayed more or less the same over the past two decades? And, therefore, is the apparently wide-spread increase in economic anxiety over this period justified or not?

Beach and Slotsve find that the chances of moving from a middle- into a lower-income group varied according to precisely which groups were being talked about. The chance of moving from anywhere up to 150 percent of the median income into the very bottom group (below 25 percent of the median) — what Beach and Slotsve call a "catastrophic income loss" — fell from 6.6 percent in 1972 to 5.1 percent two decades later. The decline was not smooth, however, as the very bottom group became relatively more important as a result of both the 1981–82 and 1990–91 recessions. By contrast, the chance of moving from below 150 percent of the median to below 75 percent of the median was higher (44.4 percent versus 40.8 percent) at the end of the two decades than at their beginning. The chances actually peaked in 1985 (at 44.3 percent) before declining with the 1980s' expansion and finally increasing again after 1989. In sum,

> the random incidence of moderate or substantial income losses has...generally increased since the 1970s, with the most rapid increases occurring between the mid-1970s and mid-1980s;...whereas the random incidence of catastrophic income losses had become considerably smaller by the later 1980s than it had been in the early 1970s. (p. 113.)

As for the decline in income suffered by people who fell into a lower-income class, "[t]he income gap measures all show a general downward drift from the 1970s until the mid- to late 1980s" (p. 113). In other words, people who fell did not fall as far:

the median income in the lower groups was closer to the median income in the upper groups than it had been. For instance, in 1972 the median income of people whose incomes were within 50 percent either way of the median was 54.3 percent higher than the median income of those who were below 75 percent of the median. But in 1992 it was only 51 percent higher. Although the different measures Beach and Slotsve look at tend to vary with the unemployment rate, their conclusion is that "a long-run trend seems to be shifting these measures of economic insecurity *down* in the 1980s compared with their generally higher values in the 1970s" (p. 113; emphasis added).

Multiplying the chance of a loss by the size of the loss if it occurs gives much the same result: "the rise of the random incidence aspect of a substantial, though not catastrophic, income fall appears important over the 1974–85 period. Overall, however, *a general downward trend persists in the income gap and composite measures of economic insecurity in family income*" (p. 113; emphasis added).

Perhaps not surprisingly, economic insecurity indexes for individuals are "much higher" than those for families. At the beginning of the two decades under examination, insecurity indexes for women were generally higher than for men. By the end of the 1972–92 period, however, "the degree of economic insecurity of men's and women's incomes had generally converged" (p. 116), a result consistent with earlier-quoted findings about the decline of polarization among female earners. As would be expected, the cyclical variation of polarization among men seems to have given rise to a similarly cyclical variation in the indexes of economic insecurity among them. These "generally increased over the 1974–84 period and then declined with the broad expansion over the rest of the 1980s, also bouncing up somewhat in the 1990–92 recession" (pp. 116, 119).

The results quoted so far are for before-tax incomes. In general, the insecurity ratios calculated with after-tax incomes are lower and show the same general pattern of development:

"The random incidence of noncatastrophic income losses...and the corresponding composite index...again show a rise between 1974 and 1984 [see Table 21]. The remaining measures, however, are dominated by the general downward shift in the insecurity indexes" (p. 114).

How can one explain the contrarian result that, measured objectively, economic insecurity was actually *lower* after the mid-1980s than it had been before? Beach and Slotsve mention several factors: the rise of multiple-earner families, which affords a greater opportunity for risk pooling within a family; the declining importance of earnings in family income, earnings being among the least stable sources of income; and the corresponding growth of government transfers, which rose from 6 percent of family income in 1971 to 13 percent in 1992. Finally, after-tax incomes display even less insecurity than before-tax incomes because,

> [with] progressive tax rates, when incomes fall, after-tax incomes fall less than proportionally and income losses are buffered by the tax system. The significant rise in income tax rates in the 1980s augments this buffering effect and thus dampens the degree of economic insecurity, (p. 116.)

which, again, is hardly the standard view people have of the 1980s. The deeper question of how to explain why perceived insecurity seems to have increased although objective insecurity apparently has not is one the authors do not address.

Are There Messages for Policymakers Here?

Beach and Slotsve begin their review and conclusions by making the case that greater inequality can be a problem for a society. If inequality occurs because some people "are advancing up the [income] distribution, especially on the basis of their own skills and effort" (p. 120), it may matter very little that the shape of that distribution changes. On the other hand, "if others are slipping down the distribution into privation and poverty, especially on the basis of changes over which they have no influence — say, technological change or trade adjustment in the labor market — these people can suffer a major loss of standard of living and economic well-being" (p. 120). The economic insecurity that results may depress aggregate demand in the economy, thus causing macroeconomic difficulty. Poverty may breed poverty in the next generation. "A more fissured, economically split society may have fewer shared values of fair process....A more economically polarized society may be a more fractious, less stable society" (p. 121). On the other hand, an excessive concern with fostering equality may lead to taxes and regulations that reduce economic growth by discouraging people from investing in "human capital" — that is, their own betterment.

Unemployment plays a crucial role in Beach and Slotsve's findings. In general, they do not believe the evidence supports the increasingly common view that Canada is becoming two societies. But where polarization has increased — among male earners, in particular — changes in the unemployment rate explain virtually the entire increase. It follows that, if Canadians wish to avoid greater income inequality, they should avoid periods of high unemployment. The $64,000 question, of course, is how to do so. Noting that a number of recent measures, such as unemployment insurance reform, aim to address problems on the supply side of the labor market, Beach and Slotsve argue that greater attention should be paid to the demand side; in other words, periods in which overall demand in the economy sags appreciably should be avoided, presumably by means of better macroeconomic management — a policy, the authors presumably would agree, that is easier to recommend than to deliver.

Another clear message emerging from Beach and Slotsve's work is that the social safety net, which includes progressive income taxation,[6] makes a difference. Their Table 17 shows very

---

6 This might be thought to undermine the current enthusiasm for a "flat tax." A flat-rate income tax may or may not be less progressive than the existing...

clearly that "market incomes" are distributed less equally than "money incomes" (that is, market incomes plus government transfers, including pensions). Money incomes, in turn, are distributed less equally than money incomes minus income taxes. In short, despite what many people evidently believe about the income tax system, both the current system of government transfers and the income tax system work in the direction of greater equality. Moreover — though this is a result that will surprise many people — both the tax and transfer systems worked *more* in the direction of equality at the end of the 1980s than at the beginning of that decade.

These results are consistent with what are now consensus findings in the literature: that inequality is not as severe in Canada as in the United States; that the premium on high-skilled labor that emerged in the United States from the late 1970s on has not been observed to such an extent in Canada; and that a likely reason for the difference in the two countries' experience is the more secure safety net provided in this country.[7]

Beach and Slotsve summarize the differences between the Canadian and US experiences in Chapter 2, in a literature review that also makes clear that the causes of inequality are not yet perfectly understood. For instance, as they report, much of the growing inequality in earnings in Canada results, not from unemployment or growing gaps in wages paid per hour, but from

---

Note 6 - cont'd.

...income tax, depending on what is included in income, but it almost certainly would not be nonprogressive. Most such plans include a generous personal exemption, which means that although the *marginal* tax rate is the same for all taxpayers, the *average* rate of tax is zero for anyone who makes less than the exemption and rises gradually — progressively — to approach the marginal rate at very high incomes.

7 It does not necessarily follow, of course, that, if spending on social programs were to be reduced in Canada, greater inequality would result. Although, on balance, public spending is redistributive, most public spending is not redistributive and some is perversely redistributive, as when university tuition is kept substantially below cost mainly for the benefit of children of the middle class and higher. On the other hand, it is obviously possible that cuts in social spending could increase inequality.

increasing differences in the number of hours worked per week. Moreover, there does not appear to be a simple sectoral explanation — for example, the decline of manufacturing — for the growth of inequality: differences in earnings have increased in virtually all sectors of the economy, a phenomenon also experienced in the United States. That inequality is far from completely understood leads Beach and Slotsve to conclude their study with a plea for more and better data:

> Specifically, we need panel data that follow workers' mobility through time in order to identify the extent to which...a shift of workers in the distribution arises from incumbent workers' losing jobs and income as they slide down the distribution or from new cohorts' entering the distribution at lower incomes than did their predecessors. Unfortunately, available Canadian data cannot answer this question. (p. 127.)

Even readers who normally are unenthusiastic about petitions for greater public expenditures may appreciate the worth of such data.

Chris Sarlo's Comments

The volume also includes comments on Beach and Slotsve's work by economists Chris Sarlo, from Nipissing University in North Bay, Ontario, and Alan Harrison, from McMaster University in Hamilton, Ontario.

Sarlo begins his comments with a general discussion of inequality, the gist of which is that "there is such a wide variety of influences, with some offsetting others, that it is quite impossible to predict changes in key measures of income inequality" (p. 162). One important influence is the age composition of the work force. Because people's income typically first rises and then falls as they age, "even in a society where every worker has exactly the same *lifetime income*, there will be quite substantial income inequality" (p. 162) at any given time. The reason is that different people will be at different stages of their life cycles. Thus "the rise in the proportion of elderly citizens in the population is likely to increase the degree of inequality, since most retirees experience a sharp reduction in income" (p. 163). Changes in the rate of marital breakdown will also cause changes in the rate of inequality. And so will changes in the distribution of and reward to skills. Because so many things determine inequality, Sarlo argues, "[i]t is not at all clear...that rising inequality, should it be detected, is a sign of increasing unfairness in society" (p. 163).

Given the many sociodemographic changes that have taken place in Canada since 1971 — the increase in the proportion of seniors, the doubling in importance of lone-parent families, the decline in average family size, the 50 percent increase in females' labor force participation rate, the cumulation of university graduates, to name just a few — it would be surprising if there had not been changes in the various measures of inequality. Yet no change is precisely what Beach and Slotsve find. As Sarlo emphasizes, "[i]t therefore bears repeating: there is *no support* for the claim that the middle class is declining, and there is *nothing to support* the view that family incomes are more unequal or more polarized now than they were 20 years ago" (p. 164; emphasis in original).

Comparing data taken directly from Statistics Canada's Survey of Consumer Finances with Beach and Slotsve's "interpolations" from its summaries of Canadian income distributions, Sarlo notes no appreciable difference between the two. On the other hand, he argues that "more research is needed to examine the consistency of the differences between the two approaches" (p. 165). In passing, he notes that in 1990 almost 160,000 families and individuals reported zero or less than zero income and were therefore classified in most reports on poverty and inequality as "the poorest of the poor" (p. 166). In fact, "those with negative incomes are invariably self-employed persons who have declared business losses against other income" (p. 166); moreover, 42 percent of the heads of these households were employed, 26 percent were homeowners, and 17 percent had university degrees.

Beach and Slotsve's main conclusions — that the polarization of female earnings has declined since the 1970s, that the increase in the polarization of male earnings can be explained by the business cycle, and that family incomes have experienced no trend, either up or down — prompt this comment from Sarlo:

> Anyone who has followed the discussion of social policy issues in recent years, especially in the popular press, will have been told repeatedly that income disparities are growing, that the rich in Canada are getting richer and the poor, poorer. This claim is made without a shred of supporting evidence, yet some journalists, commentators, and even academics continue to repeat this canard in the belief, perhaps, that it must be true since they have heard it so often. I hope, without much optimism, that these folks will look at the Beach and Slotsve study. (p. 168.)

Sarlo summarizes their finding that "there is no statistically significant trend in middle-class shares over the period" by paraphrasing Mark Twain: "reports of the demise of the middle class have been greatly exaggerated" (p. 169).

Although Sarlo regards Beach and Slotsve as having "undertaken an impressive and important study" (p. 169) that will be "a valuable resource, not only for students of inequality, but also — and perhaps most important — for journalists and commentators" (p. 164), he nevertheless criticizes what he calls their "single-minded focus on income as an indicator of well- being" (p. 169). Other contributors to well-being are in-kind social benefits and mortgage-free home ownership, "which reduces the household's required spending on housing and thereby improves the living standard over others at the same income" (p. 170), yet such items do not figure in Beach and Slotsve's calculations. The implication is that including such nonmonetary forms of income would increase the incomes of many people at the bottom end of the money-income distribution and thus change our perceptions of the social importance of changes in recorded inequality.

Sarlo would also prefer a focus on household consumption, which, by saving or borrowing, most people try to gear to their lifetime income, rather than their annual income, which can fluctuate a great deal. Using Statistics Canada data on consumption, Sarlo shows that there is considerably less inequality in family consumption than in family income. In 1982, consumption among the top fifth of consumers was four times greater than consumption among the bottom fifth, while in terms of incomes the top-to-bottom ratio was roughly ten. Nor do consumption data for 1982, 1986, and 1992 show any obvious trend in inequality. What is more, when household consumption is calculated on a per capita basis, "consumption per person in the top quintile is only about twice that in the bottom quintile" (p. 171); by this measure, at least, "inequality declined slightly over the past decade" (p. 171), a result consistent with US research that shows no significant increase in the inequality of per capita consumption. Sarlo ends his discussion of consumption by noting that ownership of various consumer durable such as color televisions, cars, and dishwashers is not greatly different across income quintiles and has become much more common at the bottom of the income distribution than it was even 15 years ago.

Sarlo concludes his comments by discussing policy issues. In his view, government transfers have, in fact, an "indeterminate effect on inequality over time," since

> redistribution...may serve to stifle both the current and future income growth of recipients....While [it] may benefit recipients in the short term,...it may well work to their long-term disadvantage. It may trap them at a lower level of income than would otherwise have been the case, leaving them with little hope of entering the mainstream of society. (p. 173.)

Beyond this, Sarlo argues it is not obvious that policymakers should be concerned with changes in the income distribution:

> Poverty is a serious problem. Unemployment is a serious problem. But changes in...polarization and inequality measures...tell us nothing about either problem....[P]eople can slip

down the income distribution curve simply by standing still. Indeed, their relative position can slip because their incomes are increasing more slowly than the average....[W]e need to know the source of the change in inequality before we make any moral judgments. (p. 174.)

Finally, Sarlo takes issue with Beach and Slotsve's recommendation that the state become more involved on the demand side of the economy in order to reduce unemployment:

Even a casual observer of government activities over the past two decades could argue that it has been precisely government policies that have reduced productivity and efficiency and contributed greatly to the slackness in the labor market. (p. 174.)

Alan Harrison's Comments

Harrison also begins his comments on Beach and Slotsve by noting the increasing frequency of public commentary about widening income inequality and the vanishing or disappearing middle class. He follows this up with the important methodological point that inequality and polarization are not the same thing. Citing a well-known result from Statistics Canada's Michael Wolfson that a distribution can actually become less unequal even as its tails become larger (which is the usual definition of polarization), he reminds us that this is exactly what happened in Canada between 1973 and 1981.

Harrison concludes his summary of Beach and Slotsve's calculations of middle-class incomes by declaring that they

have done us a great service. The debate over polarization, like many others that relate to social policy, is often characterized by a great deal of heat but not a lot of light; this study yields enough light to cast a shadow over arguments that the middle class has gone the way of the dodo. (p. 179.)

Yet Harrison does find fault with several aspects of Beach and Slotsve's approach. To begin with, like most other people doing such work, they compare

> snapshots at different points in time....[T]he data...tell us only that today's rich people, whoever they are, are relatively richer than were yesterday's rich, whoever they were....Most data are silent on whether today's and yesterday's rich (or poor) are the same people, (p. 180.)

a comment that echoes Beach and Slotsve's plea for a data series to be constructed that would follow the fortunes of individual Canadians through time.

Like Sarlo, Harrison believes information about income distributions should be supplemented with data on consumption. In particular, if, in a period of high unemployment, people

> expect an upturn in the economy, this might be reflected in their consumption behavior, which will smooth out the downturn....If, however, their incomes really are more insecure, they may attempt to live within their current means and not make plans based on a brighter future. (pp. 182–183.)

He suggests good econometric work might be able to discover whether they have been reacting to unemployment the same way in recent years as they did in the 1970s.

Finally, on the relevance of Beach and Slotsve's work to policymakers, Harrison argues that, in their own summary of their work, the authors tend to underplay the role of social policy in explaining the differences between Canadian and US experience in the 1980s. Like Sarlo, Harrison also invokes Mark Twain, arguing that, on the basis of Beach and Slotsve's findings, "the welfare state could justifiably claim that reports of its death have been greatly exaggerated" (p. 182).

William Watson

Are We Becoming Two Societies?

Chapter 1

Introduction

Canada has just come through a severe recession following a decade of dramatic change in the labor market and workers' incomes. Real incomes have not increased significantly — and in some cases have fallen substantially — in recent years. The rising tax revenues and government deficits that paid for several decades of advances in social programs are unlikely to be sustained. Burgeoning government debt, particularly at the federal level, and stalled growth in incomes have set the scene for a major social policy review (now under way in Ottawa) and marked fiscal cutbacks in the provinces. The C.D. Howe Institute's series "The Social Policy Challenge" affords a timely opportunity to review Canada's changed economic and social environment and, in turn, the roles of and needs for social programs. This study looks at one aspect of this changed environment: shifts since the 1970s in the shares of the population receiving middle-class incomes and incomes above and below the middle class, and in the proportion of total income accruing to the "poor," the "middle," and the "rich." We seek to set out the evidence of such changes in Canada as background information for evaluating the roles of social programs.

Issues Pointing to Polarization

The 1980s and its two severe recessions saw significant changes in labor markets in Canada and other industrialized countries. Employment shifted from manufacturing and goods-producing jobs to services sector jobs; from traditional heavy industry employment to jobs in new technology sectors; and from stable, full-time, full-year employment toward higher job turnover and unemployment, employer downsizing and restructuring, and increased part-time work. Higher technological requirements for jobs and the shifting of low-skill jobs offshore to low-wage Third World environments reduce the opportunities for low-skill workers in Canada. Efforts to enhance labor efficiency and shed "surplus labor" discriminate against those just entering the job market, who become the "last hired and first fired." Institutional changes such as declining real minimum wages, significantly higher taxes, rapid increases in immigration levels, and free trade agreements leave workers feeling less secure in their economic well-being.

The US labor market has gone through many similar changes that suggest the likely direction for distributional change in Canada. Numerous commentators have drawn attention to the resultant marked increase in inequality in the distribution of income in the United States. While average real family incomes rose by 8.6 percent between 1977 and 1989, this increase was not at all evenly distributed. The incomes of the lowest 20 percent of families in each year's distribution fell by 10.4 percent, while the incomes of the middle 20 percent declined by only 5.3 percent, and the incomes of the top 20 percent *rose* by 25.4 percent — with a 78.0 percent increase for the top 1 percent of families (United States 1991, 67). Changes in after-tax incomes are even more extreme.

As families and workers have moved out of the middle range and toward the two ends of the distribution, concern has been raised about the "downwardly mobile" (Wells 1993), "rising inequality in America" (Danziger and Gottschalk 1993), "the incredible shrinking middle class" (Duncan, Smeeding, and Rodgers 1992a; see also Beatty 1994), and the polarization of society (Phillips 1993). Technical surveys, major research studies, and entire issues of journals have followed.[1] US Labor Secretary

---

1 See Levy and Murnane (1992) for a technical survey. Major research studies include Levy and Michel (1991); Burtless (1990); Danziger and Gottschalk (1993). The February 1992 issue of the *Quarterly Journal of Economics* was devoted to this topic.

Robert Reich talked about seeing that country's middle class transformed into an economically "anxious class," squeezed between the wealthy and the chronically poor and trying to preserve its standard of living (Manegold 1994). The empirical literature suggests that the United States is going through a period of widening income polarization. Indeed, the phenomenon appears to be quite widespread across many western industrialized countries, with inequality changes in family incomes in Britain since the late 1970s even more marked than in the United States ("Inequality" 1994; "Slicing" 1994).[2]

Public attention in Canada has also focused on the changing job market and its implications for middle-class incomes. A series of *Globe and Mail* articles entitled "Squeezed out: The shrinking middle class" (Freeman 1990; McInnes 1990; see also Farney 1994; Greenspon 1993) have highlighted concern. Much of the public's concern has also focused on job insecurity in the middle class (see, for example, Canadian Council on Social Development 1993), the restructuring of family roles, and the increased tax burden on the middle class and others in the 1980s (Contenta 1993). But until quite recently, little work had been done on the exact nature and degree of the distributional changes going on in Canada. This study reviews the basic evidence on change in the income distribution in Canada over the past 20 years, and particularly during the 1980s. It especially examines what degree of polarization has occurred in that income distribution, the extent of a declining middle class, the distributional effect of the increased tax burden, and the basis for a feeling of economic insecurity.

Current Evidence on Distributional Change in Canada

Most of the research literature on distributional change in Canada falls into two basic strands. The first looks at shifts of

---

2 For example, between 1969 and 1992 in the United States, the ratio of the top 20 percent of household incomes to the bottom 20 percent increased from 7.5 to 11; in Britain between 1977 to 1991, this multiple rose from 4 to 7.

employment and the associated changes in wages, particularly
for young workers and for employment growth in the service
sector of the economy.[3] Since services sector jobs tend to be spread
over a broader range of wages and skill requirements than
blue-collar manufacturing jobs, the industry/occupation shift toward services (the so-called deindustrialization of employment)
widens earnings inequality in the economy. These analyses have
produced such results as the following:

- For the economy as a whole, the employment share of high-
  skill occupations increased by nearly seven percentage points
  over the 1971–86 period. The share of employment of the
  low-skilled group also increased, though at a much smaller
  rate. But the medium-skilled group saw its share of employment decline by more than seven percentage points (Economic Council of Canada 1990b).

- Between 1981 and 1986, job growth in Canada was concentrated at the very bottom and in the upper-middle regions of
  the wage distribution. The result was a modest decline in the
  share of employment in the middle of the distribution, and
  a larger decline in the lower-middle region (Myles, Picot, and
  Wannell 1988a, 4.2).

- Change in the industrial and occupational mix of jobs has
  occurred mainly among young people, who have relatively
  undeveloped labor market skills and who face the full force
  of shifting labor demand. The most dramatic change has
  been a downward shift in the distribution of wages of workers ages 16 to 24. This downward shift has been widespread,
  occurring in all industrial sectors, occupational groups, regions, and levels of education (Myles, Picot, and Wannell
  1988a, 4.3).

---

3 See, for example, Baldwin and Gorecki (1993); Betts and McCurdy (1993);
   Economic Council of Canada (1990a); Myles (1987); Myles, Picot, and Wannell
   (1988a, 1988b)

- The occupational redistribution that occurred during the 1980s, while substantial, appears to account for relatively little of the total change in the wage distribution. Wage changes occurring *within* industry and occupation groups had the main impact on the wage distribution (Myles, Picot, and Wannell 1988a, 4.2; 1988b, 8). Broader factors than just industry/occupation shifts appear to be at work in the labor market.

- Even less important in explaining changes in wage inequality in the 1980s are changes in the composition of the work force by age, gender, and educational attainment (Richardson 1994). Supply-side changes in the labor market do not appear to be the major factors in understanding the changes seen in the 1980s, in contrast to the previous two decades. Demand-side factors operating across a broad spectrum of the economy seem the more likely source for explanations.

The second strand of Canadian studies on distributional change focuses more specifically on the trends in and polarization of the annual earnings of individual workers and on evaluating various explanations for observed patterns of change.[4] Since hourly wages times annual hours worked yields total earnings, one would expect the above patterns in wages to carry through to the total earnings of workers — and that is indeed the case, though with some interesting wrinkles. Some illustrative results follow:

- Earnings inequality rose in Canada in the 1980s for both men and women working full time all year. It increased markedly during the sharp 1981–82 recession and never returned to its pre-1981 level during the subsequent expansion of the 1980s. This suggests that significant structural

---

4 See, for example, Beach and Slotsve (1994); Betcherman and Morissette (1993); Burbidge, Magee, and Robb (1994); Dooley (1986, 1987); Leckie (1988); Morissette, Myles, and Picot (1994a, 1994b); Wolfson and Murphy (1993)

changes took place in the labor market during the early to
mid-1980s (Morissette, Myles, and Picot 1994a, 13).

- Canada ended the 1980s with earnings inequality at substantially higher levels than in the 1970s. Between 1979 and
  1989, two years at the peak of their respective business
  cycles, earnings inequality variously measured increased by
  at least 12 percent for both men and women (Morissette,
  Myles, and Picot 1994b, 3).

- The increase in earnings inequality in the labor market can
  be traced to two trends that date back to the 1970s: a
  downward drift in the real and relative earnings of workers
  at the bottom end of the distribution (the working poor), and
  a widening gap in annual earnings between younger and
  older workers in the labor market (Morissette, Myles, and
  Picot 1994b, 1).

- Three phases of change can be identified in the earnings
  polarization for workers in Canada. From 1967 to 1984,
  polarization of men's earnings generally increased; from
  1984 to 1989, it trended downward; and from 1989 to 1991,
  it began increasing again as the effects of the 1990–92
  recession cut in. Compared with polarization changes in the
  earnings of males in the United States, Canadian results are
  only about a third as strong. When attention is restricted to
  full-time, full-year workers, women show a much more
  marked pattern of earnings polarization change than do
  men. Among full-time, full-year workers, women's earnings
  polarization increased between 1984 and 1989, but at only
  about half the rate of increase experienced by men (Beach
  and Slotsve 1994, 333).

- Changes in earnings differentials across education groups in
  Canada (for example, between high school and university
  graduates) play a very modest role in explaining rising
  earnings inequality. In contrast, changes in the age distribution of earnings (for example, between young people entering

the labor force and more experienced middle-aged workers) have been relatively profound (Morissette, Myles, and Picot 1994b, 7).

- Wage inequality has an important cyclical component that causes it to increase during recessions and decrease during expansions; in Canada, it also trended upward between 1981 and 1992 (Richardson 1994, abstract).

- Part of the rise in earnings inequality in Canada in the 1980s came from a growing polarization in weekly hours and annual hours worked in the labor market. A "declining middle" in the distribution of hours worked gave rise to a declining middle class in the earnings distribution among men (Morissette, Myles, and Picot 1994a, 13–14). Both the percentage of earners working more than 40 hours a week and the percentage of earners working fewer than 35 hours a week increased over the 1981–89 period, while the percentage working 35 to 40 hours a week declined by 11 percent for men and by 7 percent for women.

Researchers have devoted considerable debate to establishing the principal explanations for such results. So far, the discussion has focused almost exclusively on the US experience. Levy and Murnane (1992) review the alternative explanations in the US literature quite comprehensively. Broadly speaking, four major hypotheses have been advanced to explain the recent findings on earnings inequality, earnings polarization, and skill differentials (for a more extensive review than provided here, see Beach and Slotsve 1994, sec. 5).

The Deindustrialization/Opening Economy Hypothesis holds that growing international competition is driving the production of manufactured goods previously carried out by high-wage, often unionized, workers in North America offshore to lower-wage countries. There is thus a decreased demand for relatively low-skilled workers, who then shift into lower-paying, low-skilled services sector jobs. Rationalization of production following the

Canada-US Free Trade Agreement may have hastened this effect in Canada. High-skilled technicians, analysts, and professionals, on the other hand, are seeing the market for their expertise widen to reflect an international demand, pushing their earnings up. There is likely some truth to this argument, but it cannot explain why industry/occupation shifts alone do not account for much of the increased earnings inequality, although most of the change appears to be within industry/occupation categories.

A second explanation, the Technological Change Hypothesis, argues that new technological advances such as chip-based and information-transfer technologies have resulted in the replacing of many production-line workers and middle-level white-collar workers by both lower-skilled support service workers and high-skilled technicians and professionals. This approach provides some explanation for both the widening skill differentials by age and education level observed in the United States and the marked increase in earnings inequality within industry/occupation groups noted above. Much of the recent US literature credits such technological change as the primary demand-side explanation. However, few studies are directly able to measure technology and identify which sectors are experiencing the fastest adoption of such change; hence, the conclusion remains only tentative (Berman, Bound, and Griliches 1994; Bound and Johnson 1992). Nor can this hypothesis account for several other findings: Why did the education differential in earnings not widen significantly in Canada in the 1980s the way it did in the United States? Why is much of the increased inequality and polarization of earnings in Canada due to polarization in hours worked, while that does not appear to be the case in the United States (where polarization of wage rates is the determining factor)? And why does the rate of increase in earnings polarization in Canada appear to be significantly lower than that in the United States?

The third set of explanations may be collectively referred to as the Relative Supply Changes Hypothesis. According to the literature that proposes these ideas, the supply of workers with university degrees is a critical determinant of college-high school earnings differentials. In the 1980s, the increased demand for college-educated workers was met by a decelerating increase in supply in the United States but by a continuing substantial increase in Canada. Hence, the education premium for university graduates did not rise significantly in Canada, whereas it did in the United States (Dooley 1986; Freeman and Needels 1993). At the same time, the increased move of women, especially married women, into full-time employment and into higher-paying jobs may have reduced job opportunities for men around the middle regions of the earnings distribution for full-time, full-year workers. Other factors that may have limited the growth of earnings inequality in Canada compared with that in the United States include faster growth of real gross domestic product during the expansion of the 1980s, a better external trade balance, and less Canadian exposure to low-skilled legal and illegal immigration than the United States experienced over the period.

The evidence appears to support aspects of all three hypotheses. Clearly, however, much more work needs to be done to discriminate among these major explanations with Canadian data.

A fourth set of explanations offered for the US situation, perhaps best called the Deregulation Hypothesis, points to various government policies implemented in the 1980s to facilitate competition and the working of market forces. Real minimum wages fell, as did many welfare benefits; the fraction of the work force that was unionized declined dramatically (Card and Freeman 1993; "Inequality" 1994; "Rich Man, Poor Man" 1993; "Slicing" 1994). In Canada, however, while some deregulation measures were brought in, the unionization rate did not decline; indeed, total transfer income rose in Canada. The Deregulation Hypothesis would thus appear to be less relevant in Canada than the first three hypotheses.

But the earnings of individual workers, which are what we have been looking at so far, are not the sole determinant of the total income of families. Family income is the basis of household consumption expenditures and wealth accumulation. It also serves as the conventional proxy for the economic well-being of the household's members. The so-called middle class is also conventionally defined in terms of family income. The major source of family income is typically the earnings of family members in the labor market — 78 percent of family income in 1992 (Statistics Canada, cat. 13-207, 1993, 90).[5] But the majority of families nowadays have more than one earner,[6] so a relevant factor is how the earnings of spouses match up within a household. For example, do high-earning husbands tend to marry low-earning wives? The evidence suggests not. Over the past 15 years, the correlation of husbands' and wives' earnings has been positive (that is, high earners tend to marry high earners, while low earners marry low earners) and has been rising noticeably.[7] Even if no one's earnings changed, if high-earning men marry high-earning women and low-earning men marry low-earning women, that could increase the overall inequality of family incomes. Changing household structures in recent decades could be a further reason for a widening distribution of family incomes, as households have become more polarized between growing proportions of two-earner families at the upper end of the distribution and of no-earner or part-time-earner single-parent families (particularly those headed by single mothers) near the bottom end. The dramatically rising labor market involvement of women in Canada over the past 30 years would tend to shift the distribution of family incomes away from that of men's earnings (which was the major determinant 30 years ago) toward

---

5 This figure has been declining: in 1971, it was 88 percent, but by 1980 it had dropped to 83 percent.

6 The mean number of earners per family in Canada rose from 1.55 in 1967 to 1.75 in 1980; it peaked at 1.80 in 1989, but thereafter declined with the 1990–92 recession, to 1.70 in 1992 (Statistics Canada, cat. 13-207, 1993, 19).

7 Blackburn and Bloom (1994, tables 2 and 4) estimate that, between 1979 and 1987, the simple correlation of husbands' and wives' earnings (among married-couple families) rose from 0.10 to 0.18 in the United States and from 0.06 to 0.21 in Canada).

a more complex pooling of incomes across earners and other income recipients in the household. Family income also includes sources other than just earnings. In 1990, 6 percent of the income of families came from investment sources; 11 percent on average came from various government transfers.[8] The proportion of family income from transfers has risen noticeably over the past 20 years.

In this study we go beyond the distribution of workers' earnings to examine total incomes, of individuals and of families. Specifically, how have recent changes in distribution shown up in the distribution of family incomes? How have family incomes before and after taxes trended over time, and how have families withstood recessions and prospered through economic expansions? The literature on the distribution of family incomes in Canada is far more limited than that for the first two strands of literature discussed above.[9] The family is where most of us live, so it is important to find out what has happened to family income inequality. Indeed, the only two recent studies on family income distribution change in Canada (Blackburn and Bloom 1993; McWatters and Beach 1990), did not address the issue of polarization of family incomes in Canada, so few results are available. The objectives of this study are thus to review the basic evidence on income polarization among families and on income changes in the middle class in Canada, especially in the 1980s; to examine the distributional effect of income taxes and the distribution of disposable income over the period; and to investigate any impact of increased polarization on economic insecurity among Canadian families.

It may be useful to highlight several of the study's major findings here, before setting out the details at length. The answer

---

8 The proportion of family income from transfers increased steadily over the years from 6 percent in 1971 through 7.5 percent in 1980 to 13 percent in 1992 (Statistics Canada, cat. 13-207, 1993, 90).

9 See, for example, Blackburn and Bloom (1993); Henderson and Rowley (1977, 1978); Horner and MacLeod (1980); Love and Poulin (1991); McWatters and Beach (1990); Rashid (1989); Sharpe (1993); Wolfson (1986, 1989).

to the question posed by the study's title, "Are We Becoming Two Societies?" is "no," but we do appear to have come through two periods of widening polarization in labor markets during the past two decades — the first between about 1975 and 1985, and the second more recently, following the 1990–92 recession — that may generate growing concern. There has been a marked difference in polarization patterns and income changes between men and women over the past 20 years in Canada, though in recent years polarization changes in women's incomes have started to resemble those of men. There is a highly significant cyclical sensitivity in the degree of income polarization at the lower end of the income distribution. Finally, the proportion of individuals and families considered to be middle class has fallen since 1989–90, and middle-class incomes have also fallen since 1989 for individual men and for families.

The study is organized as follows. Chapter 2 provides basic comparative evidence for the United States and Canada. Chapter 3 examines the polarization of individuals' earnings and incomes; then Chapter 4 examines family incomes and the evidence for a declining middle class. Concerns about disposable income and economic insecurity are addressed in Chapter 5. Finally, Chapter 6 presents conclusions and observations on social policy concerns in an era of increased polarization.

Chapter 2

Background Evidence for the United States and Canada

Comparison of Family Income Inequality Changes in Canada and the United States

To provide a basis of comparison, we begin this study with some background evidence on family income inequality changes in the United States. Blackburn and Bloom (1993) compare the changes in the income distribution of families and unattached individuals that occurred in Canada and the United States over the 1979–87 period. Some of their results are provided in Table 1. A distribution can be divided into the poorest 20 percent of households, the next poorest 20 percent, and so on, up to the highest-income 20 percent of households; the five resulting segments are called the quintile groups of the distribution. The table's top panel presents the corresponding shares of income for each of these quintile groups in the distribution.

It is immediately evident from Table 1 that different patterns of changes have occurred in Canada and the United States. Family income inequality is generally higher in the United States than in Canada. In the United States, bottom-income shares fell ("the poor got poorer"), top-income shares rose ("the rich got richer"), and the middle quintile's share (one measure of the middle class) declined slightly. These results are also illustrated in the top panel of Figure 1. In the case of Canada, the top quintile's share also rose, while the middle quintile's share declined slightly as well; but the bottom quintile's share increased over the period — a pattern that illustrates the increasing role of transfers in the Canadian economy, since transfers have their predominant effect at the lower end of the income distribution.[1] While the proportion of income in the form of transfers for family units rose slightly from 11.4 percent to 12.0 percent in the United States between 1979 and 1987, it shot up from 10.4 percent to 15.1 percent in Canada. As a result, the United States experienced an unambiguous increase in family income inequality over the period, but Canada did not follow suit. However, when these various shifts in income shares are combined into the summary measures of inequality found in the second panel of Table 1, they register a reduction in inequality for Canada. (For further details on specific definitions of the three summary inequality measures in Table 1, see the Appendix.)

Family incomes can also be expressed in per capita terms (as total family income per person in the family) to better represent the distribution of income resources *per person* across individuals in the economy. When family incomes are expressed in per capita terms, the results (shown in the third and fourth panels of Table 1 and in the bottom panel of Figure 1) indicate an unambiguous *reduction* in family income inequality in Canada over the 1979–87 period.[2] These results should be contrasted with those on total family earnings (shown in the bottom two panels of Table 1). The distribution of family earnings (which are pooled across multiple earners in those households where more than one earner resides) shows unambiguous and marked increases in inequality in both countries and to approximately the same degree. The big difference in family income patterns between the two countries has reflected the enhanced role of transfers in Canada. Indeed, "the

---

1 Attributing this increase in the bottom-income share predominately to the greater role of transfers in the Canadian economy follows from the work of Blackburn and Bloom (1993) and especially from Blank and Hanratty (1993); Dooley (1994); Phipps (1994); Ross, Shillington, and Lochhead (1994); and Vaillancourt (1994).

2 Unambiguous changes in inequality are based on the Lorenz dominance criterion, whereby one Lorenz curve (or set of cumulative income shares) lies uniformly above another.

Table 1: *Family Income Inequality Indicators,*
United States and Canada, 1979 and 1987

	United States		Canada	
	1979	**1987**	**1979**	**1987**
Family Income Quintile Shares				
Bottom quintile	3.9%	3.5%	4.3%	4.8%
2nd quintile	10.0	9.6	10.8	10.8
3rd quintile	17.1	16.7	18.0	17.4
4th quintile	25.8	26.0	25.9	25.5
Top quintile	43.2	44.2	41.0	41.5
Family Income Inequality Measures				
Mean log deviation	.425	.466	.348	.295
Entropy index	.263	.278	.229	.222
Gini coefficient	.398	.411	.373	.371
Per Capita Income Shares				
Bottom quintile	5.0%	4.2%	6.3%	6.7%
2nd quintile	11.2	10.6	12.0	12.4
3rd quintile	16.7	16.5	17.0	17.0
4th quintile	24.0	24.4	23.7	23.6
Top quintile	43.1	44.3	41.0	40.3
Per Capita Inequality Measures				
Mean log deviation	.336	.387	.253	.213
Entropy index	.249	.273	.202	.187
Gini coefficient	.380	.401	.346	.335
Family Earnings Quintile Shares				
Bottom quintile	3.8%	3.5%	4.4%	3.9%
2nd quintile	11.1	10.4	12.2	11.4
3rd quintile	17.9	17.4	18.6	18.1
4th quintile	25.7	26.0	25.5	25.8
Top quintile	41.5	42.7	39.3	40.8
Family Earnings Inequality Measures				
Mean log deviation	.366	.402	.310	.338
Entropy index	.239	.258	.208	.230
Gini coefficient	.379	.395	.352	.371

Note: "Families" refers to families and unattached individuals in this table.

Source: Blackburn and Bloom 1993, various tables.

Figure 1:   *Family Income Shares and Per Capita Income Shares,*
United States and Canada, 1979 and 1987

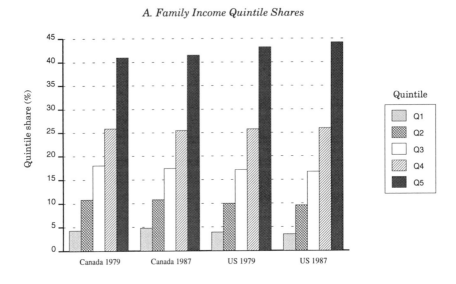

A. *Family Income Quintile Shares*

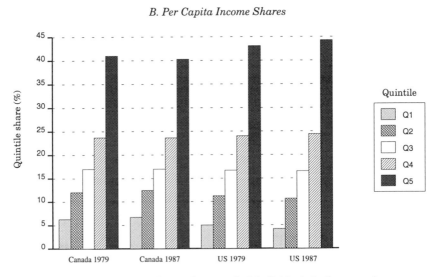

B. *Per Capita Income Shares*

Note: "Families" refers to families and unattached individuals in these graphs.

Source: Blackburn and Bloom 1993.

**Figure 2: *Changes in Income Inequality
among Families, United States, 1947–90***

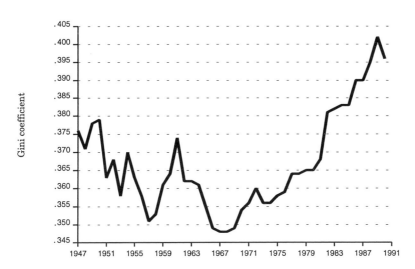

Source: Karoly 1993, figure 2.1.

chief empirical finding of the [entire volume of studies that includes the Blackburn and Bloom paper] is that Canadian labor market and income support policies mitigated against the 1980s trend of rising inequality that swept the United States" (Card and Freeman 1993, 9).

Inequality changes over a longer span of time in the United States are shown in Figure 2 in terms of the frequently used Gini coefficient of family incomes.[3] (The Appendix explains the Gini coefficient as perhaps the most widely used summary measure of income inequality.) As can be seen, family income inequality generally narrowed in the 1960s but then widened quite dramatically, so that, by the late 1980s, it was historically large by post-World War II standards.

---

3 The Gini coefficient values in Figure 2 are for "families" alone and do not include unattached individuals, whereas the figures in Table 1 are for "family units" and do include unattached individuals.

Figure 3: *Changes in Income Inequality among*
Families, by Percentile Relative to
Median Income, United States, 1963–89

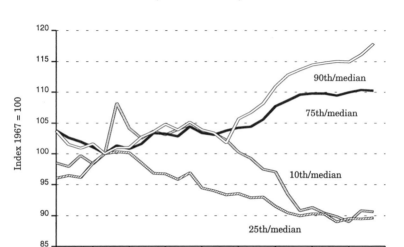

Source: Karoly 1993, figure 2.3.

Another perspective on the spreading out of the US family income distribution is provided in Figure 3, which shows the trends in various percentile income levels (that is, the income level that divides the distribution so that a certain percentage have incomes at or below this level, and the remainder have incomes above it) relative to the median or middlemost income in the distribution. Compared with a base of 100 in 1967, the upper-income ratios have risen since the late 1960s, while the lower-income ratios have drifted down. Evidently, family incomes have been spreading out toward both the bottom and the top ends of the income distribution.

Cross-sectional data such as the Current Population Surveys (CPSs) in the United States, however, cannot tell us how families and individuals move up or down in the distribution from one year to the next. They show only how families and individuals *in the same relative position* in the distribution fare between years. To identify movements of *given* families and individuals between regions of the distribution, we must examine panel data (which track the same individuals or households over a period of time) such as that collected by the Panel Study of Income Dynamics (PSID) for the United States. Duncan, Smeeding, and Rodgers (1992b) use the PSID data for the 1967–86 period to examine year-to-year shifts of given households among the low-income, middle-income, and high-income regions of the distribution (the dividing lines are given real income levels that correspond approximately to the 20th and 90th percentiles of after-tax household incomes). Over this period, they find that the share of adults in the middle group (a measure of the middle class) declined from 75 percent in 1978 to 67 percent in 1986. The average percentage of individuals exiting the middle class and moving upward ("climbing out") was 6.7 percent per year; those exiting downward ("falling out") constituted an average of 7.0 percent annually (exit rates are taken from ibid., 13). Duncan, Smeeding, and Rodgers (1992b) also find that these exit rates increased in the 1980s. Before 1980, the exit rates were 6.3 percent and 6.2 percent, respectively; from 1980 on, they accelerated to 7.5 percent and 8.5 percent, respectively. The rate of downward exit appears to have increased more markedly.

Background Trends in the Canadian Income Distribution

Next, consider background trends in the Canadian income distribution. Table 2 presents figures on mean and median real family income (in constant 1991 dollars) in Canada since 1965.[4] (Henceforth in this study, the term "families" refers to family units of

---

4 The data in Tables 2 and 3 are directly reported by Statistics Canada (cat. 13-207, various issues) and are not based on interpolation calculations by the authors. The series used in this study do not go back beyond 1965 because the population covered and the income sources covered were slightly different before then. The coverage and definition of economic family used in this study have essentially been constant since then. Table 2 refers to "families" rather than "family units" (which were the basis of Table 1).

Table 2: *Mean and Median Family Incomes, Canada, Selected Years 1965–92*

	Mean	Median
	(constant 1991 dollars)	
1965	32,095	29,016
1967	34,760	31,262
1969	37,553	33,723
1971	41,017	36,978
1972	42,696	39,171
1973	44,577	40,430
1974	46,915	42,750
1975	47,433	43,014
1976	50,480	45,044
1977	49,449	45,523
1978	50,564	46,197
1979	50,159	46,162
1980	51,793	47,870
1981	50,881	46,532
1982	49,728	44,827
1983	49,550	44,057
1984	48,851	43,934
1985	50,032	44,796
1986	52,045	46,515
1987	52,709	46,964
1988	53,670	47,921
1989	55,443	49,218
1990	54,528	48,652
1991	53,131	46,742
1992	52,880	47,094

Source: Statistics Canada, cat. 13-207, various issues; current incomes have been converted to constant 1991 dollars by the authors (based on the consumer price index).

Figure 4: *Mean and Median Real Family Incomes, Canada, 1965–92*

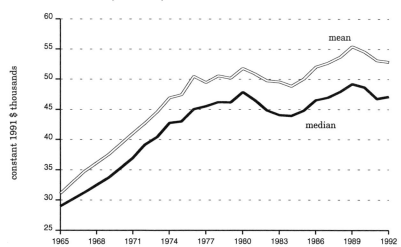

Sources: Statistics Canada, cat. 13-207, various issues; and authors' calculations (the conversion of current incomes to constant 1991 dollars, based on the consumer price index).

two or more persons and thus does not include unattached individuals.) The two series are also graphed in Figure 4. The median of a family income distribution is the middlemost income level, or that level of income for which half of all families have incomes below it and half have incomes equal to or above it. The mean is simply the average income across all families. As in any distribution that has a long right-hand tail with a small proportion of very high incomes (as illustrated by Appendix Figure A-2), the mean is pulled up by these top incomes so that it always lies above the median. The main thing to note is the flattening of the growth in real family incomes over the period, especially in the 1980s. For example, the average rate of growth in median family incomes was 4.01 percent from 1965 to 1971, 2.65 percent from 1971 to 1980, 0.44 percent from 1980 to 1992, and 0.15 percent from 1986 to 1992.[5] The falloff in growth of incomes is clearly evident in

---

5 Corresponding rates for mean income are 4.07 percent, 2.47 percent, 0.71 percent, and 0.24 percent, respectively.

Figure 4, along with the decline in real incomes following the major recessions early in the 1980s and at the end of that decade. Note also that the limited increase in family incomes since the mid-1970s has been obtained while more earners in the household have spent time working to keep up family incomes. Median family income peaked in 1980, then declined; not until 1988 did it surpass that peak, and by 1992 it had again fallen below its 1980 level.

Since the earnings patterns of men and women differed significantly over the period, Table 3 provides similar income figures for individual male and female income recipients. Here the differences are quite marked. Men's real incomes peaked in 1976 and had not regained that peak by 1992. Their average annual growth rate in median incomes was 1.33 percent in the 1970s (1972 to 1980) and an average decline of 0.50 percent in the 1980s (1980 to 1992). Women's real incomes, on the other hand, rose fairly steadily over the period, with median incomes rising by 3.78 percent in the 1970s and by 2.08 percent in the 1980s. When we control for cyclical changes in incomes, the average growth in median incomes over the 1972–92 period was 2.5 percent a year for women and 1.2 percent a year for family income; no growth occurred in men's incomes (Appendix Tables A-1 and A-8).[6] Men's incomes were also harder hit by the two recessions that bookended the 1980s. Women's incomes are on average still markedly below those of men (partly because of significantly lower wages per hour and partly due to a shorter average number of hours worked), but the ratio of women's median incomes to men's median incomes rose from 32 percent to

---

6 It should be noted that the regression procedure used to separate out underlying trend and cyclical effects possibly underestimates any trend effects. The cyclical indicator, the adult male unemployment rate, while a conventional indicator of cyclical activity, itself generally trended upward between 1972 and 1992. The part of the effect attributed to cyclical fluctuations may also incorporate a trend component. Thus, any trend effects estimated by the regression procedure could involve a slight underestimate.

Table 3:   *Mean and Median Incomes of*
             Individual Income Recipients, Canada, 1971–92

	Men		Women	
	Mean	**Median**	**Mean**	**Median**
		(constant 1991 dollars)		
1971	27,709	25,102	11,663	7,932
1972	28,841	26,453	12,253	9,057
1973	29,482	26,702	12,634	9,665
1974	30,835	27,928	13,458	10,204
1975	31,022	28,264	13,671	10,493
1976	33,025	29,316	14,041	10,439
1977	31,238	29,102	14,969	11,415
1978	31,315	28,453	15,237	11,493
1979	31,329	28,563	15,190	11,451
1980	31,450	28,603	15,478	11,566
1981	30,950	28,031	15,916	12,170
1982	30,045	26,528	15,875	12,038
1983	29,431	25,049	15,642	11,436
1984	29,015	25,047	16,056	12,063
1985	29,827	25,567	16,272	12,441
1986	30,105	25,760	16,700	12,930
1987	30,103	25,716	16,957	13,240
1988	30,682	26,430	17,298	13,457
1989	31,260	26,865	18,068	14,408
1990	30,740	26,675	18,237	14,481
1991	29,820	25,357	18,040	14,215
1992	29,632	25,259	18,500	14,291

Source: Statistics Canada, cat. 13-207, various issues; current incomes have been converted to constant 1991 dollars by the authors (based on the consumer price
index).

Figure 5: *Mean Real Incomes of Men*
and Women, Canada, 1971–92

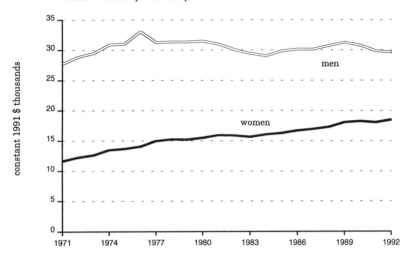

Sources: Statistics Canada, cat. 13-207, various issues; and authors' calculations (the
conversion of current incomes to constant 1991 dollars, based on the consumer
price index).

57 percent over the period. The quite different patterns of income
growth are illustrated in Figure 5.

Table 4 provides a more detailed breakdown of the data in
the family income distribution for selected years since 1972. Each
intersection of a row and a column contains a pair of numbers:
the first is the mean income level for a given decile or 10 percent
group of families, ranked from the lowest-income to the highest-
income decile groups, while the second (shown in parentheses) is
the share of total income received by that decile group. Peak
incomes occurred in 1989, just before the severe recession of
1990–92. The ratio of top-decile means to bottom-decile means is
approximately 10:1. The last column of the table contains the percentage change for each decile's means between 1980 and 1992.
Growth in the mean or median incomes for a distribution clearly
hides quite different changes over different regions of the distribution. The bottom and top regions experienced real income gains
in the 1980s, while the middle and lower-middle regions lost out

Table 4: Decile Mean Real Family Income and Decile Shares of Families, Canada, Selected Years 1972–92

(constant 1991 dollars; figures in parentheses are decile shares in percentages)

Decile	1972	1976	1980	1982	1984	1986	1988	1990	1991	1992	% Change 1980–92
Bottom	8,728 (2.0)	10,655 (2.1)	10,926 (2.1)	11,485 (2.3)	10,557 (2.2)	11,998 (2.3)	12,719 (2.4)	12,442 (2.3)	12,152 (2.3)	12,080 (2.3)	10.6
2nd	17,008 (4.0)	19,701 (3.9)	20,639 (4.0)	20,392 (4.1)	19,338 (4.0)	21,064 (4.0)	22,181 (4.1)	22,309 (4.1)	21,604 (4.1)	21,569 (4.1)	4.5
3rd	24,389 (5.7)	27,816 (5.5)	29,316 (5.7)	27,658 (5.6)	26,225 (5.4)	28,582 (5.5)	29,808 (5.6)	30,151 (5.5)	28,895 (5.4)	28,607 (5.4)	-2.4
4th	30,797 (7.2)	35,409 (7.0)	36,704 (7.1)	34,983 (7.0)	33,677 (6.9)	35,918 (6.9)	37,295 (6.9)	37,714 (6.9)	35,984 (6.8)	35,916 (6.8)	-2.1
5th	36,543 (8.6)	42,067 (8.3)	43,885 (8.5)	41,596 (8.4)	40,546 (8.3)	42,930 (8.2)	44,393 (8.3)	45,028 (8.3)	43,228 (8.1)	43,292 (8.2)	-1.4
6th	41,630 (9.8)	48,453 (9.6)	50,760 (9.9)	48,434 (9.7)	47,343 (9.7)	50,040 (9.6)	51,803 (9.7)	52,449 (9.6)	50,662 (9.5)	50,827 (9.6)	-0.1
7th	47,232 (11.1)	55,665 (11.0)	57,947 (11.3)	55,872 (11.2)	54,596 (11.2)	57,835 (11.1)	59,779 (11.1)	60,507 (11.1)	58,907 (11.1)	58,840 (11.1)	1.5
8th	54,306 (12.7)	64,441 (12.8)	66,721 (13.0)	64,921 (13.1)	63,399 (13.0)	67,102 (12.9)	69,521 (13.0)	70,537 (12.9)	68,722 (12.9)	68,600 (13.0)	2.8
9th	65,311 (15.3)	77,192 (15.3)	79,372 (15.4)	84,755 (17.0)	76,774 (15.7)	80,152 (15.4)	85,471 (15.9)	85,059 (15.6)	83,329 (15.7)	83,155 (15.7)	4.8
Top	101,020 (23.7)	123,402 (24.4)	118,258 (23.0)	107,180 (21.6)	116,050 (23.8)	124,828 (24.0)	123,729 (23.1)	129,083 (23.7)	127,829 (24.1)	125,913 (23.8)	6.5

Source: Statistics Canada, cat. 13-207, various issues; figures have been calculated using an interpolation program designed by the authors (see Beach and Slotsve 1993 for details).

in both relative and absolute terms. The shares for the bottom and top quintiles rose from 6.1 percent and 38.4 percent, respectively, in 1980 to 6.4 percent and 39.5 percent in 1992, while the second and third quintiles' shares fell from 12.8 percent and 18.4 percent, respectively, to 12.2 percent and 17.8 percent over the same period. Alternatively stated, the ratio of the bottom-decile mean to the median rose by 12 percent in the 1980s, and the ratio of the top-decile mean to the median rose by 8 percent. This is a rather different pattern from that illustrated in Figure 3 for the United States, where top-decile incomes rose while bottom-decile incomes fell. Again, the increased role of transfers at the bottom end of the Canadian income distribution appears to have had a substantial effect in offsetting earnings losses and increased earnings inequality.

Chapter 3

Individual Incomes

We turn now to the principal issue of this study: Has there been an increased polarization in incomes in Canada? This chapter examines individuals' incomes. Family incomes, which typically pool income receipts across individuals in a household, are examined in Chapter 4.

Data, Concepts, and Methodology

Source data for most of this study come from Statistics Canada's *Income Distributions by Size in Canada* (cat. 13-207), which has been published annually since 1971. Ideally, one would like to use actual survey observations on the individual respondents to the Survey of Consumer Finances (SCF), on which these publications are based. But since such individual data are generally unaffordable and hence inaccessible to researchers in Canada, an alternative methodology has been developed for this study that instead uses detailed income distribution tables (as illustrated in the Appendix)[1] from the annual publications. We wrote a computer program that takes as input the published tables or histograms of income for any group and the published mean and median income levels for the group, and, by interpolation procedures, computes as output all the various measures of polariza-

---

1 Because the actual microdata are not available, this study cannot analyze per capita income distribution or distributions that involve multiple dimensions such as gender, age, and education together. Consequently, this report analyzes and highlights broad trends in the income distribution over time.

tion, decile shares, and middle-class shares used in this study.[2]
Since the results are derived through interpolation, they contain
a certain degree of "noise" and simple random fluctuations. Emphasis will thus be placed on general trends and persistent
patterns in the results through time rather than on individual
numbers for a single year. Also, critical to the approach is a
reasonable number of income intervals in the histograms over
which the interpolation can be performed. Since the number of
such intervals in the tables on incomes increased from eight to
nineteen in 1972, we report interpolation-based results only for
the years since 1972. It should also be noted that, until 1977,
Statistics Canada did not provide imputations for missing income
responses, although it has done so since 1977 (Statistics Canada,
cat. 13-207, 1979, 30–31). Thus, there may be a slight degree of
noncomparability of income distribution series before and after
this year. Consequently, we focus on distributional changes in the
1980s, though we provide some historical coverage back to the
early 1970s.

The issue of income polarization is still sufficiently recent
that there is no agreement on a single way to measure it. More
formal analysis has been provided by, for example, Foster and
Wolfson (1993) and Esteban and Ray (1994). Intuitively, polarization may be best thought of as a complement to inequality that
highlights a specific form of distributional change. The latter
measure highlights how relative incomes change within a distribution — as illustrated most directly, say, by decile or quintile
income shares, the Lorenz curve, or the Gini coefficient. Polarization, on the other hand, focuses on proportions of persons or
population shares over different regions of a distribution.
Changes in inequality capture any general changes in relative
incomes across all regions of a distribution. A change in polarization, however, refers to a particular form of distributional shift

---

2 For technical details of the programs and procedures used, see Beach and
   Slotsve (1993), appendix A,

that involves changes in the population shares at the two ends of the distribution. A more polarized distribution has a larger proportion of the population in the two tails. Appendix Figure A-3 illustrates how a distributional change can increase polarization while leaving overall inequality unchanged, by shifting population from the middle-upper and middle-lower regions of the distribution into both the middle and the two ends. Measures of the size of the middle class typically reflect the proportion of the population within some specified middle region of the distribution. If the distributional change involves a population shift out of the middle regions of the distribution and into the two tails, then both inequality and polarization will increase. This is the pattern that evokes concern about a dwindling middle class, especially if the shift is predominantly from the middle end to the bottom end of the distribution. This type of shift is also consistent with the first two broad hypotheses discussed in Chapter 1. The poverty rate, for example, is a form of polarization measure, in that it involves the proportion of the population with incomes below some poverty line or low-income cutoff.

How, then, does one distinguish among the bottom, middle, and top regions of a distribution to implement polarization measures? One approach would involve dividing the distribution according to absolute (real) dollar cutoffs into low-income, middle-income, and high-income regions. For example, cutoffs of $15,000 and $50,000 (in constant 1991 dollars) could be used to divide the distribution of family incomes into lower, middle, and upper regions. Such cutoffs, however, quickly become out of date as the distribution shifts over time. Most authors therefore favor expressing the cutoffs in relative terms, as a percentage or multiple of the median or midpoint of the distribution. For example, the Economic Council of Canada (1990a, 14) considers plus or minus 25 percent of the median; see also Sharpe (1993, 6), who uses 74 percent to 125 percent of the median, and Wolfson (1989, 13), who uses 75 percent to 150 percent of the median. Kosters and Ross (1988) use plus or minus 50 percent of the median, and

Bluestone and Harrison (1988) employ cutoffs of 50 percent and 200 percent of the median of a distribution. In the latter case, then, anyone with income below 50 percent of the median is considered to be in the low-income group, anyone with income more than twice the median is classified as in the high-income group, and the rest belong to the middle-income group. If one is interested in highlighting the middle-class region in the analysis, one can opt for narrower percentages around the median; if one wishes to focus on polarization issues, one may choose percentage cutoffs that are further from the median level. Note also that this approach allows one to compute the income share for each (lower, middle, and upper) region along with the population share, so that a corresponding degree of inequality can be examined as well.[3]

To capture robust patterns of polarization change, we use a range of alternative polarization measures:

- polarization index 1: the share of income recipients in the distribution with incomes beyond 50 percent of the median income level (that is, below 0.5 of the median and above 1.50 of the median);
- polarization index 2: the share of recipients below or above 75 percent of the median;
- the population share of recipients below 25 percent of the median;
- the population share below 50 percent of the median;
- the population share above 150 percent of the median;
- the population share above 175 percent of the median;
- the population share above 200 percent of the median.

Note that, when distributional groups are divided in terms relative to the median, the bottom-, middle-, and upper-income

---

3 Note, however, that since the number of persons in each region can change over time, relative income shares between regions are not equivalent to relative mean incomes between regions. Only when the regions are expressed in quintile terms (for example, bottom quintile, middle 60 percent of persons, and top quintile of a distribution) do the two become equivalent.

groups can each be characterized by both income shares (the proportion of total income in the population that is received by members of the group) and population shares (the proportion of the population that occurs in each group). When the distribution is divided into equal-population-sized decile groups, as in Table 4, only the income shares vary between decile groups. Dividing the distribution relative to the median allows a more informative characterization of polarization in a distribution.

Finally, the measure of income used in this study is Statistics Canada's definition of total income: "money income from wages and salaries, net income from self-employment, investment income, government transfer payments, pensions and miscellaneous income" (Statistics Canada, cat. 13-210, 1992, 34). Since it is restricted to money income, it does not include implicit rent on owner-occupied housing, unrealized capital gains, any income in kind, or market valuation of housework done.

Polarization of Individual Earnings

By far the major source of income for most individuals in the economy is their annual earnings obtained from working in the labor market. Earnings consists of wage and salary income in the case of paid workers, and net self-employment income for the self-employed. Chapter 1 highlighted a number of major changes that have occurred in the earnings distribution for women and men since the 1970s.[4] Figure 6 illustrates the pattern of real (1991 dollar) mean earnings of men and women from 1971 to 1992. As can be seen, women's mean earnings were substantially below men's and rose fairly steadily over the period, except in the recessions at the beginning and end of the 1980s. The higher

---

4 The data on earnings distributions on which the results of this section are based come from Statistics Canada, *Earnings of Men and Women* (cat. 13-217, 1994 and earlier years). The data used refer to "All Earners."

Figure 6: *Mean Real Earnings of Men and Women, Canada, 1971–92*

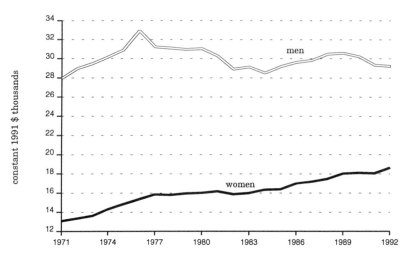

Sources: Statistics Canada, cat. 13-217, various issues; and authors' calculations (the conversion of current incomes to constant 1991 dollars, based on the consumer price index).

mean earnings of women reflect both rising real wages and longer average hours worked in the labor market. The higher mean earnings of men, in contrast, had fallen by 1992 substantially below their 1976 peak. They fell fairly steadily from 1976 to 1984, picked up during the expansion of the 1980s, and thereafter declined again through the 1990–92 recession. The earnings gap between men and women clearly narrowed during the 1970–92 period, but the narrowing was due partly to falling men's earnings, not just to rising women's earnings.

Has polarization changed in the earnings distribution as well? Here we follow and extend earlier work (Beach and Slotsve 1994).[5] Tables 5 and 6 provide polarization results for the earnings of men and women, respectively, for selected years from 1971,

---

5 The reported years during the 1970s in Tables 5 and 6 are selected to be comparable to the polarization results in Beach and Slotsve (1994, table 3).

Table 5: Alternative Polarization Measures for All Male Earners, Canada, Selected Years 1971–92

	1971	1975	1979	1981	1982	1984	1985	1986	1987	1988	1989	1990	1991	1992
Polarization Indexes (percent)														
1 (± 50% of median)	48.8	48.2	49.6	50.3	55.3	58.5	57.7	55.8	56.5	54.7	54.0	55.3	57.5	59.3
2 (±75% of median)	29.4	30.6	31.7	30.6	35.7	37.9	37.6	35.6	36.0	34.3	32.9	35.3	36.9	39.1
Population Shares														
Below 0.25 of median	15.5	14.4	15.0	15.3	17.5	18.1	17.2	16.8	16.8	16.3	15.1	16.1	16.8	18.1
Below 0.50 of median	25.4	24.6	25.6	26.6	28.5	29.5	29.1	28.5	28.3	27.4	27.3	27.8	29.0	29.7
Above 1.50 of median	23.4	23.6	24.0	23.8	26.8	29.0	28.7	27.3	28.3	27.3	26.7	27.5	28.5	29.6
Above 1.75 of median	13.9	16.2	16.7	15.3	18.3	19.8	20.4	18.9	19.3	18.0	17.8	19.2	20.1	21.0
Above 2.00 of median	11.0	13.1	12.5	9.9	11.8	13.0	13.8	12.8	12.8	11.9	11.9	13.5	14.2	15.1
Income Shares														
Below 0.25 of median	1.57	1.51	1.61	1.71	1.86	1.90	1.81	1.78	1.76	1.73	1.62	1.71	1.78	1.86
Below 0.50 of median	5.01	4.98	5.32	5.67	5.60	5.70	5.72	5.74	5.60	5.44	5.71	5.58	5.79	5.68
Above 1.50 of median	46.9	47.0	46.5	46.6	52.8	56.7	56.4	53.8	55.3	53.7	53.0	54.5	56.4	58.2
Above 1.75 of median	32.5	36.1	35.5	33.5	40.0	43.2	44.4	41.3	42.1	40.0	40.0	42.5	44.2	45.8
Above 2.00 of median	27.5	30.7	28.0	23.9	28.9	31.8	33.3	31.0	31.3	29.7	30.1	32.9	34.5	35.9

Source: Statistics Canada, cat. 13-217, various issues, table 1; figures have been calculated using an interpolation program designed by the authors (see Beach and Slotsve 1993 for details).

Figure 7:   *Polarization Indexes for*
Men's Earnings, Canada, 1971–92

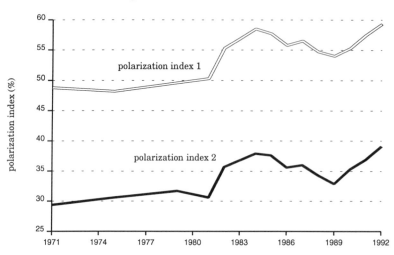

Source: Statistics Canada, cat. 13-217, various issues; figures have been calculated using
         an interpolation program designed by the authors (see Beach and Slotsve 1993
         for details).

with more detailed coverage for the 1980s up to 1992. The two
polarization indexes — one is for the percentage of workers with
earnings beyond plus or minus 50 percent of the median, and the
other is for the percentage with earnings beyond plus or minus
75 percent of the median — appear in the upper panel of each
table. So, for example, in 1992, 59.3 percent of male workers are
estimated to have had earnings that lay beyond plus or minus
50 percent of the median. In the case of men, the degree of
polarization changed very little through the 1970s, but then
jumped up quite markedly in 1982–84 following the sharp recession of the early 1980s; it drifted down through the extended
expansion of the 1980s (though not back down to its pre-1982
level), and then shifted up again in the 1990–92 recession. This
pattern is illustrated in Figure 7. Clearly, the 1980s and early
1990s were a far more volatile period of polarization change than
the 1970s.

Table 6: Alternative Polarization Measures for All Female Earners, Canada, Selected Years 1971–92

	1971	1975	1979	1981	1982	1984	1985	1986	1987	1988	1989	1990	1991	1992
							(percent)							
Polarization Indexes														
1 (± 50% of median)	65.2	62.2	64.1	63.4	65.3	65.8	65.0	63.1	64.3	62.5	60.7	61.6	63.1	64.6
2 (± 75% of median)	45.5	40.0	43.2	41.4	43.6	44.6	43.7	42.0	43.2	41.5	39.4	40.7	42.2	44.0
Population Shares														
Below 0.25 of median	21.0	19.0	19.1	17.4	17.7	17.4	17.4	16.6	16.9	16.7	16.2	15.7	16.2	17.2
Below 0.50 of median	33.1	31.9	31.6	30.9	31.5	31.1	31.1	30.1	30.1	29.8	29.2	28.8	29.3	30.3
Above 1.50 of median	32.2	30.3	32.6	32.6	33.8	34.7	34.0	33.0	34.2	32.7	31.5	32.8	33.8	34.3
Above 1.75 of median	24.5	21.0	24.0	24.0	25.9	27.2	26.2	25.4	26.4	24.7	23.2	25.0	26.0	26.9
Above 2.00 of median	17.0	15.0	17.6	17.9	19.4	20.9	20.0	18.9	20.5	18.2	16.5	18.2	18.9	20.4
Income Shares														
Below 0.25 of median	2.13	2.01	1.89	1.88	1.87	1.78	1.80	1.75	1.73	1.75	1.73	1.65	1.68	1.78
Below 0.50 of median	5.97	6.31	5.84	6.05	6.05	5.80	5.82	5.87	5.64	5.73	5.76	5.68	5.69	5.74
Above 1.50 of median	63.8	59.4	63.6	62.9	65.3	67.2	66.1	64.0	66.2	63.7	61.3	63.2	64.7	66.0
Above 1.75 of median	53.0	45.8	51.7	50.9	54.6	57.2	55.8	53.5	55.8	52.9	49.9	52.7	54.2	56.0
Above 2.00 of median	40.7	35.6	41.2	41.0	44.4	47.6	46.2	43.3	46.8	42.5	39.3	41.9	43.0	46.0

Source: Statistics Canada, cat. 13-217, various issues, table 1; figures have been calculated using an interpolation program designed by the authors (see Beach and Slotsve 1993 for details).

Figure 8: *Polarization Indexes for*
Women's Earnings, Canada, 1971–92

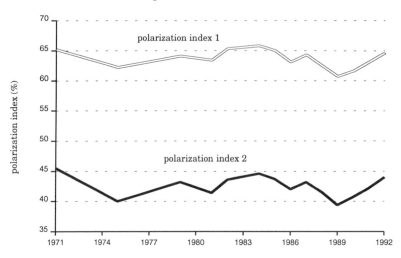

Source: Statistics Canada, cat. 13-217, various issues; figures have been calculated using
an interpolation program designed by the authors (see Beach and Slotsve 1993
for details).

Polarization rates for women earners (see the top panel of
Table 6) are substantially higher than those for men, at least
partly because of the wider differences in hours worked by women.
Thus, in 1992, 64.6 percent of women workers are estimated to
have had earnings beyond plus or minus 50 percent of the median. The results, illustrated in Figure 8, show a more noticeable
downward drift in polarization rates in the 1970s for women than
for men. Beginning in the 1980s, the pattern of polarization
change for women became generally similar to that for men,
although the amplitude was not as marked: between 1981 and
1992, polarization rates increased by 1.2 to 2.6 percentage points
for women, but by 8.5 to 9.0 percentage points for men.[6] Evi-

---

6 If 1979 is used as the initial year of comparison, the increases are 0.5 to 0.8 of
a percentage point for women versus 7.4 to 9.7 percentage points for men.
Since polarization rates are lower for men, the increases when expressed in
relative terms are even more marked for men than for women.

dently, the phenomenon of increased polarization since the 1980s has been a much more important issue for men than for women. Interestingly, though, the sharp increase in polarization in the 1990–92 recession was felt by women and men to approximately the same extent.

Can one identify the source of polarization changes in earnings? The polarization indexes are the percentages of workers at both the bottom end and the top end of the earnings distribution. The second or middle panels of Tables 5 and 6 show those two portions separately. So, for example, in the last column of Table 6, the first polarization rate figure (64.6 percent) can be seen to be the sum of the 30.3 percent of women workers with earnings below 50 percent of the median and the 34.3 percent whose earnings were above 150 percent of the median. For women, the relatively small change in overall polarization rates hides different patterns of change in the lower- and upper-earnings groups. More workers moved into the higher-earnings group (which increased by 1.7 percentage points between either 1979 or 1981 and 1992), while workers were also moving out of the lower-earnings group (which decreased by 0.6 to 1.3 percentage points between 1979 or 1981 and 1992). Thus, women's earnings distribution was characterized by upgrading at both ends.

For men, in contrast (see Table 5), the marked increased in overall polarization rates arose from the increased proportion of workers at both the upper and lower ends. Of the 9.7 point increase in the first polarization rate between 1979 and 1992, 4.1 points resulted from workers' slipping down to the bottom earnings range and 5.6 points arose from workers' shifting up into the higher earnings range.[7] Thus, about one-third to two-fifths of polarization increases for men between 1979 and 1992 arose from downgrading or slippage in earnings, while more than half came

7 If 1981 is used as the initial year of comparison, the figures are 3.1 points and 5.8 points, respectively.

from upgrading of earnings as workers moved into the upper regions of the distribution.

The group most negatively affected by the increased polarization of earnings is thus the 3 to 4 percent higher proportion of men who find themselves further down the distribution, in the lower-earnings group, than had previously been in that group. Their reduced earnings are accentuated further by the fall in median earnings that also occurred over the period. Note that this earnings slippage between two years such as 1981 and 1992 could have arisen from either or both of two shifts: individuals' moving down the distribution as higher-paying jobs were replaced by lower-paying work and intermittent spells of unemployment, and young workers' entering the distribution at a lower level than their predecessors had. Estimating the degree to which this increase in the lower-population share is due either to slippage of older cohorts or to new cohorts' being worse off than their predecessors would require panel data that follow given individuals over several years. Such data are only now beginning to be collected for Canada. Note also that the shifting of workers into both the upper and lower ends of the distribution, as evidenced for men, is consistent with both the Deindustrialization/Opening Economy Hypothesis and the Technological Change Hypothesis discussed in Chapter 1. For women, however, other factors appear to have been at work at the lower end of the earnings distribution, where the shifts are more likely related to higher wages for women and to the growing attachment of women to the labor market.

The bottom panels of Tables 5 and 6 present sets of income shares, which are more useful in illustrating inequality changes in the earnings distribution. Briefly, it can be seen that, for both men and women, upper-income shares during this period generally reflect what happened to upper-population shares — shifting up dramatically during the 1982–85 period, drifting down over the following expansion, and then moving up again during the recession of the early 1990s. Lower-income shares show a far less systematic pattern.

Figure 9: *Polarization Indexes for Men's Income, Canada, 1972–92*

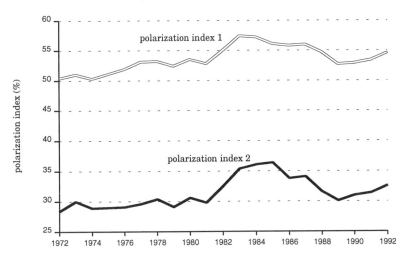

Source: Statistics Canada, cat. 13-207, various issues; figures have been calculated using an interpolation program designed by the authors (see Beach and Slotsve 1993 for details).

Polarization of Individual Incomes

Consider now the total incomes of individuals, not just their earnings. Since people can receive income without earning in the labor market — for example, in the form of income assistance or pensions — the population of individuals with incomes is broader than that of earners. What, then, does one find about the polarization of individuals' incomes in Canada? The top panel of Table 7 shows the polarization indexes for men's incomes from 1972 to 1992. As can be seen, the degree of income polarization generally drifted up during the 1970s, but — as with the degree of earnings polarization — increased sharply early in the 1980s (following the 1981–82 recession); it then gradually decreased to a trough in 1989 and started rising again with the 1990–92 recession. This pattern is illustrated in Figure 9. The basic pattern of increased

Table 7: Alternative Polarization Measures for Male Income Recipients, Canada, Selected Years 1972–92

	1972	1974	1976	1978	1980	1981	1982	1983	1984	1985	1986	1987	1988	1989	1990	1991	1992
Polarization Indexes (percent)																	
1 (± 50% of median)	50.4	50.3	51.9	53.2	53.5	52.8	55.0	57.4	57.2	56.1	55.8	56.0	54.7	52.7	52.9	53.4	54.6
2 (± 75% of median)	28.4	28.9	29.1	30.4	30.6	29.8	32.5	35.4	36.1	36.4	33.8	34.1	31.6	30.1	31.0	31.4	32.6
Population Shares																	
Below 0.25 of median	13.5	12.4	12.6	13.0	13.1	12.1	12.3	12.7	12.7	11.9	11.7	12.0	11.5	10.4	11.6	10.9	11.5
Below 0.50 of median	26.1	25.7	26.1	27.2	27.1	26.5	26.6	26.9	27.0	26.0	25.6	25.5	25.1	24.3	25.2	24.8	25.2
Above 1.50 of median	24.3	24.6	25.8	26.0	26.4	26.3	28.3	30.5	30.3	30.1	30.2	30.5	29.5	28.3	27.7	28.6	29.4
Above 1.75 of median	14.9	16.5	16.6	17.4	17.5	17.7	20.2	22.7	23.3	24.6	22.1	22.1	20.1	19.8	19.4	20.5	21.1
Above 2.00 of median	10.1	13.7	11.3	10.8	11.5	13.7	16.4	18.9	18.9	19.7	14.7	15.3	14.5	13.0	13.9	14.9	15.6
Income Shares																	
Below 0.25 of median	1.62	1.47	1.45	1.50	1.44	1.35	1.28	1.28	1.25	1.21	1.21	1.26	1.25	1.13	1.27	1.16	1.14
Below 0.50 of median	5.87	5.87	5.88	6.19	6.20	6.22	6.01	5.87	5.92	5.80	5.71	5.62	5.66	5.67	5.70	5.64	5.60
Above 1.50 of median	48.4	49.2	51.5	51.1	51.4	51.1	54.9	58.9	58.2	57.9	57.9	58.3	56.5	54.8	54.4	56.1	56.9
Above 1.75 of median	34.5	37.5	38.3	38.5	38.4	38.5	43.3	48.2	48.6	50.2	46.7	46.7	43.2	42.8	42.7	44.9	45.4
Above 2.00 of median	26.3	32.8	29.7	27.2	28.2	31.8	37.1	42.2	41.5	42.4	34.8	35.9	34.2	32.0	33.8	36.0	36.8

Source: Statistics Canada, cat. 13-207, various issues; figures have been calculated using an interpolation program designed by the authors (see Beach and Slotsve 1993 for details).

polarization over the 1970s and a sharp increase in the early 1980s did not continue beyond the middle 1980s, when an abatement set in with the broad expansion of the economy. The reversal brought rates down, but only to about their 1981 values — still above polarization rates in the early to mid-1970s. We essentially find a pattern similar to that seen in the 1980s for earnings polarization, though the changes are more damped than they were for earnings. Not surprisingly, changes in earnings are the principal factors driving the changes in polarization rates for total incomes.

To what extent are the polarization changes driven by factors at the bottom or top ends of the distribution? The middle panel of Table 7 again shows the proportions of individuals at the two ends. Clearly, the patterns of changes in the lower- and upper-population shares are rather different and, until about 1989 (with the 1990–92 recession taking hold), upward shifts — that is, shifts toward the top end of the distribution — dominated overall polarization changes. For example, over the 1981–85 recession-and-recovery period, the proportion of men with incomes above 175 percent of the median rose from 17.7 percent to peak at 24.6 percent, while the proportion with incomes below 25 percent of the median rose from 12.1 percent to 12.7 percent, and then fell back to 11.9 percent. Over the longer 1981–92 period, the percentage of the population with income beyond plus or minus 50 percent of the median rose by 1.8 percentage points. This is the sum of a 1.3 percentage point decline in the lower-income group and a 3.1 percentage point rise in the upper-income group. Again, transfers probably dampened major changes toward the bottom end of the distribution and may even have reversed the trend in the bottom-population share of earnings. Polarization changes at the top end of the distribution generally reflect the same pattern as found for earnings — rising from 1972 until 1983–85, drifting down until 1989–90, and then shifting up with the onset of the 1990–92 recession, though not nearly as much as for earnings. Year-to-year fluctuations at the lower end of the distribution are far less distinct. Over the period as a whole, though, we find that the lower-population shares trended downward slightly, whereas the upper shares increased significantly: in 1972 the shares below 25 percent of the median and above 175 percent of the median were of roughly similar size (13.5 percent versus 14.9 percent, respectively), but by 1992 the top share was almost twice the size of the bottom one (11.5 percent versus 21.1 percent, respectively).

The pattern of income shares (see the bottom panel of Table 7) generally follows that of polarization changes. Over the period as a whole, the share of total income received by the group with incomes below 25 percent of the median trended down, from 1.62 percent in 1972 to 1.14 percent in 1992 (a 30 percent decline), while the income share of the group with incomes above 175 percent of the median rose, from 34.5 percent to 45.4 percent (a 32 percent increase). If one concentrates on the critical 1981–85 period, one notes that the income share of this bottom group fell by 10 percent (from 1.35 percent to 1.21 percent) while the income share of this top group rose by 30 percent (from 38.5 percent to 50.2 percent). The population shares for these two groups, however, declined by 2 percent (from 12.1 percent to 11.9 percent) and increased by 39 percent (from 17.7 percent to 24.6 percent), respectively, over this period. The decline of the bottom group's income share is thus being driven by the group's declining incomes over this period, whereas the rise in the top group's income share is being generated primarily by the dramatic inflow of more men into the upper-income group. Clearly, different factors are at work at the two ends of the distribution.

Income polarization results for women are presented in Table 8. The first thing to notice is that, while the degree of polarization is again higher for women than for men, the difference has been narrowing. As also illustrated in Figure 10, both polarization indexes have markedly decreased since 1976; the strong downward trend has clearly dominated any cyclical pattern. It is this strong downward trend that has been narrowing

Figure 10: *Polarization Indexes for*
Women's Income, Canada, 1972–92

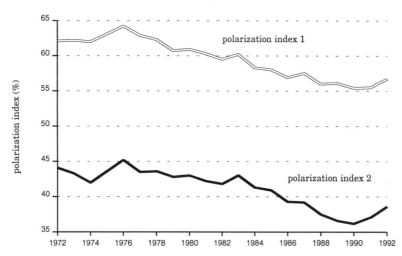

Source: Statistics Canada, cat. 13-207, various issues; figures have been calculated using
an interpolation program designed by the authors (see Beach and Slotsve 1993
for details).

the difference in polarization rates between women and men.
This pattern may reflect such major ongoing trends as the growing labor attachment of women (as more women become full-time
workers in the labor market) and the rising wages of women in
the market. It may also reflect the increased role of transfer
income to women, particularly those with dependent children,
over this period — a factor that would tend to raise the lower end
of the income distribution for women more than that for men.
Indeed, it may again be that the increased role of transfers
explains why the polarization of women's *earnings* over this
period shows only a relatively slight and irregular decrease,
whereas the polarization of *incomes* has markedly declined — so
that, while the degree of polarization of women's incomes at the
beginning of the period is approximately the same as that for
women's earnings, it ends up by the end of the period being
distinctly lower than the degree of polarization of earnings.

Table 8: Alternative Polarization Measures for Female Income Recipients, Canada, Selected Years 1972–92

	1972	1974	1976	1978	1980	1981	1982	1983	1984	1985	1986	1987	1988	1989	1990	1991	1992
								(percent)									
								Polarization Indexes									
1 (± 50% of median)	62.1	62.0	64.2	62.3	60.9	60.3	59.5	60.2	58.3	58.0	56.9	57.5	56.0	56.1	55.4	55.5	56.7
2 (± 75% of median)	44.1	42.0	45.2	43.6	43.0	42.2	41.8	43.0	41.3	40.9	39.3	39.2	37.5	36.6	36.2	37.1	38.6
								Population Shares									
Below 0.25 of median	14.5	13.1	14.9	14.9	13.9	13.8	13.4	13.8	13.4	13.4	12.2	12.7	11.3	11.8	11.1	11.1	11.9
Below 0.50 of median	26.5	26.6	27.7	26.7	25.4	25.5	24.7	25.1	24.3	24.4	23.7	24.5	22.9	23.6	23.1	23.1	23.5
Above 1.50 of median	35.6	35.5	36.5	35.6	35.4	34.8	34.8	35.1	34.0	33.6	33.2	33.0	33.1	32.5	32.3	32.4	33.3
Above 1.75 of median	29.6	28.9	30.3	28.7	29.1	28.4	28.4	29.2	27.9	27.5	27.1	26.6	26.2	24.8	25.1	26.0	26.8
Above 2.00 of median	24.1	22.7	24.6	22.6	23.4	22.3	22.9	24.0	22.9	21.8	21.3	20.7	20.0	19.2	19.6	20.0	21.0
								Income Shares									
Below 0.25 of median	1.31	1.17	1.39	1.36	1.19	1.26	1.27	1.22	1.18	1.21	1.15	1.19	1.07	1.15	1.09	1.08	1.09
Below 0.50 of median	4.60	5.03	4.95	4.65	4.45	4.60	4.50	4.35	4.24	4.39	4.53	4.71	4.50	4.72	4.74	4.68	4.51
Above 1.50 of median	69.6	68.0	70.6	68.8	68.4	67.1	66.9	68.6	66.5	65.5	64.2	64.1	63.6	62.4	61.9	62.4	64.2
Above 1.75 of median	62.4	59.8	63.1	60.4	60.7	59.1	59.0	61.5	59.0	58.0	56.6	55.9	54.9	52.5	52.7	54.3	56.1
Above 2.00 of median	54.7	51.1	55.2	51.7	52.7	50.4	51.2	54.5	52.0	49.8	48.2	47.4	45.9	44.2	44.4	45.4	47.7

Source: Statistics Canada, cat. 13-207, various issues; figures have been calculated using an interpolation program designed by the authors (see Beach and Slotsve 1993 for details).

Turning to the middle panel of Table 8, one can also see that polarization changes for women are driven primarily by changes in the bottom-population shares. Over the period as a whole, the population share for the group with incomes below 50 percent of the median fell by 3.0 percentage points, and the population share for the group with incomes above 150 percent of the median declined by 2.3 percentage points. Both shares peaked in 1976 and then decreased fairly steadily until 1989–90. That is, for women, the predominant factors driving polarization change are at work at the lower end of the distribution, while for men, as we have already seen, the predominant factors appear to be operating at the upper end of the distribution. For women, transfers appear to have a very important role, whereas for men, upward mobility — a shift toward higher incomes — appears to be quite important.

Income shares for the bottom and top groups also trended down in the 1980s. Between 1981 and 1992, for example, the income share of the group with incomes below 25 percent of the median declined by 13 percent (from 1.26 percent to 1.09 percent), and income share of the group with incomes above 175 percent of the median fell by 5 percent (from 59.1 percent to 56.1 percent). The corresponding declines in population shares were 14 percent (from 13.8 percent to 11.9 percent) and 6 percent (from 28.4 percent to 26.8 percent). The changes in income shares can be largely accounted for just by changes in polarization alone.

To what extent can one identify the underlying role of trend and cyclical factors in the income polarization results? Multiple regression is a statistical technique commonly used in economics to distinguish among several determining factors in explaining changes in some variable, such as polarization rates. Regression results on the polarization indexes and on the upper- and lower-population shares for men and women are presented in Appendix Table A-3. It can be seen that cyclical factors are basically driving the income polarization rate for men, whereas the downward trend is clearly the predominant effect for women. For example, a 1.0 percentage point increase in the unemployment rate is estimated to increase men's income polarization by 1.0 percentage point and women's by 0.37 of a percentage point. When we control for cyclical factors, polarization rates for men are not estimated to change significantly over the 1972–92 period, while for women, the estimated decline is half a percentage point per year, or 10.2 percentage points over the full period. Comparing these results with similar regressions for workers' earnings (see Appendix Table A-2), one finds that the cyclical effects on the polarization of incomes are considerably damped, and the trend effects are more strongly toward reduction of polarization (Beach and Slotsve 1994, 336). Indeed, the significant upward trend in the polarization of men's earnings is fully nullified when one looks at the distribution of total incomes. Once again, the dampening effect of transfer income appears. For example, a 1.0 percentage point rise in the unemployment rate is estimated to increase men's earnings polarization by 1.35 percentage points (versus 1.00 for income polarization) and women's by 0.87 of a percentage point (versus 0.37 for income). The regressions for the upper- and lower-population shares simply supplement these findings by confirming earlier results: the weakest cyclical effect occurs at the lower end of the distribution for women (where transfers play a critical role), and the downward trend in women's income polarization is occurring significantly at both the bottom and top ends of the distribution.

Income gains and losses over the past 20 years have also not been experienced evenly across different demographic or skill groups in the labor market. As shown in Table 9, the most marked differences are between age groups: for both women and men, increases in incomes have been largest among older income recipients and lowest among the young. Indeed, during the 1980s, both men and women in the youngest age group experienced real income losses. In the case of education, the highest income gains were obtained by those with university degrees and the lowest gains by those with the least education. One can interpret age as

Table 9: *Changes in Mean Individual Incomes by Age and Education Groups, Canada, 1972–91 and 1980–91*

	1972–91	1980–91
	(percentage change)	
	Women	
Age group		
20–24	9.2	– 8.8
25–34	31.9	3.6
35–44	53.6	18.9
45–54	54.8	19.5
65–69	60.9	12.6
70 and over	67.7	29.6
Education group		
0–8 years of education	n.a.	5.9
Completed high school	31.9	n.a.
Postsecondary certificate	n.a.	4.0
University degree	33.6	20.9
	Men	
Age group		
20–24	– 9.9	– 5.6
25–34	– 10.3	– 17.5
35–44	– 3.5	– 10.7
45–54	7.3	– 2.3
65–69	25.8	3.7
70 and over	67.3	19.0
Education group		
0–8 years of education	n.a.	– 18.1
Completed high school	– 4.7	n.a.
Postsecondary certificate	n.a.	– 8.3
University degree	– 1.9	0.3

n.a. = not available because of changes in education categories over the period.

Note: Over the 1972–91 period, women's mean incomes rose by 47 percent and men's by 3 percent. Over the 1980–91 period, the corresponding changes were 17 and – 5 percent.

Figures could not be readily updated to 1992 because of the published categories of the Statistics Canada data for 1992.

Source: Statistics Canada, cat. 13-207, various issues.

capturing labor market experience: in most cases, older workers have more skills at getting things done. What is found then is that the elderly and those with higher skill levels clearly have been the principal winners over this period, while the young and the relatively unskilled have been the major losers. Age-income profiles over a worker's career steepened during the 1980s as the real wages of starting workers fell, peak-age earnings rose (due to the increased demand for higher skills in the economy), and the real incomes of the elderly (primarily from transfers and pensions) rose relative to those of the young.

In summary, polarization rates for men and women show quite different patterns. For men, polarization rates drifted up slowly over the 1970s, then accelerated markedly during the early 1980s' recession; a reversal occurred after 1985 as polarization rates drifted down during the expansion of the 1980s, but the rates increased again in the 1990–92 recession. More than half of the increased earnings polarization for men has been due to a population shift toward the upper end of the earnings distribution. One-third to two-fifths of the increase has been due to a population shift toward the lower end of the distribution. Cyclical factors appear to be driving the changes in men's polarization rates, with no significant long-run trend evident in overall polarization rates. For women, income polarization has decreased markedly since 1976, with significant reductions occurring at both the lower and the upper ends of the distribution. The strong downward trend clearly dominates any cyclical pattern and is likely due to the growing labor market attachment of women and the increased role of transfers during the 1970s and 1980s. Polarization patterns in earnings for both men and women appear much sharper and more marked than those in income, where the patterns are more damped. Among different demographic or skill groups, one finds that, during the 1980s, young cohorts of workers experienced real income losses, while peak-age earners, the university-educated, and the elderly experienced the greatest real income gains.

The Incomes of
Middle-Class Workers

The converse of the degree of polarization can be thought of as the (population) share of the middle class. While the middle class is conventionally expressed in terms of families, it is still of interest to examine the share of the middle class in terms of individual income recipients (as reflected, for example, in such expressions as "the proportion of middle-class jobs").

Just as one can use several measures of polarization, one can also consider several estimates of the middle-class share. We consider five in this report, corresponding to population shares:

- between 0.85 and 1.15 of the median;
- between 0.75 and 1.25 of the median;
- between 0.50 and 1.50 of the median;
- between 0.25 and 1.75 of the median;
- between 0.25 and 2.00 of the median.

Tables 10 and 11 present figures for each of these measures — for women and men, respectively — for the 1972–92 period.

Results for women are provided in Table 10. The wider the measure, the larger the share of middle-class income recipients. For example, in 1992, 22.6 percent of income recipients had incomes within 25 percent of the median, while 43.3 percent had incomes within 50 percent of the median. Corresponding to the downward trend in polarization rates among women, all the middle-class share measures show a distinct upward trend. This pattern is confirmed in the regression results in Appendix Table A-4, which show that, controlling for cyclical factors, women's middle-class share trended upward by a little over one-third of a percentage point a year. Over the 20-year period from 1972 to 1992, this shift amounts to an increase of 7.3 percentage points. This systematic increase is illustrated in Figure 11 for the mid-range measure of plus or minus 50 percent of the median ($MC_{.5}$). Cyclical factors do not appear to affect women's middle-class

Table 10: Middle-Class Shares for Female Income Recipients, Canada, Selected Years 1972–92

	1972	1974	1976	1978	1980	1981	1982	1983	1984	1985	1986	1987	1988	1989	1990	1991	1992
							(percent)										
Population Shares																	
0.85 to 1.15 of median	9.8	10.8	9.9	9.9	11.7	11.5	12.0	13.2	13.5	13.7	14.2	13.8	13.6	13.7	13.4	13.9	13.1
0.75 to 1.25 of median	18.8	19.0	16.7	17.3	19.6	20.0	21.1	22.2	22.3	22.6	23.5	22.2	22.5	22.5	23.3	23.7	22.6
0.50 to 1.50 of median	37.9	38.0	35.8	37.7	39.1	39.7	40.5	39.8	41.7	42.0	43.1	42.5	43.9	44.0	44.6	44.5	43.3
0.25 to 1.75 of median	55.9	58.0	54.8	56.4	57.0	57.8	58.2	57.0	58.7	59.1	60.7	60.8	62.5	63.4	63.8	62.9	61.4
0.25 to 2.00 of median	61.4	64.2	60.4	62.5	62.7	63.9	63.8	62.2	63.7	64.8	66.5	66.6	68.6	69.0	69.4	68.9	67.2
Income Shares																	
0.85 to 1.15 of median	7.3	8.1	7.3	7.4	8.6	8.7	9.0	9.5	10.0	10.3	10.9	10.7	10.4	10.8	10.5	10.8	10.0
0.75 to 1.25 of median	13.5	14.0	12.1	12.7	14.2	14.8	15.5	15.6	16.2	16.9	17.8	16.9	17.0	17.5	17.9	18.3	16.9
0.50 to 1.50 of median	25.8	27.0	24.5	26.5	27.2	28.3	28.6	27.1	29.3	30.1	31.2	31.2	31.9	32.9	33.4	32.9	31.3
0.25 to 1.75 of median	36.3	39.0	35.5	38.2	38.1	39.6	39.7	37.2	39.8	40.8	42.3	42.9	44.1	46.4	46.2	44.7	42.8
0.25 to 2.00 of median	44.0	47.7	43.4	46.9	46.1	48.4	47.5	44.3	46.9	49.0	50.7	51.4	53.0	54.7	54.5	53.5	51.2

Source: Statistics Canada, cat. 13-207, various issues; figures have been calculated using an interpolation program designed by the authors (see Beach and Slotsve 1993 for details).

Table 11: *Middle-Class Shares for Male Income Recipients, Canada, Selected Years 1972–92*

	1972	1974	1976	1978	1980	1981	1982	1983	1984	1985	1986	1987	1988	1989	1990	1991	1992
							(percent)										
Population Shares																	
0.85 to 1.25 of median	15.7	16.7	15.7	14.4	14.4	14.5	13.8	12.1	12.1	12.9	12.9	13.1	13.8	13.9	14.3	13.8	13.5
0.75 to 1.25 of median	25.9	26.9	25.6	23.9	23.9	23.8	22.7	20.6	20.6	21.5	21.5	21.7	22.7	23.1	23.9	23.1	22.6
0.50 to 1.50 of median	49.6	49.7	48.1	46.8	46.5	47.2	45.0	42.6	42.8	43.9	44.2	44.0	45.3	47.3	47.1	46.6	45.4
0.25 to 1.75 of median	71.6	71.1	70.9	69.6	69.4	70.2	67.6	64.6	63.9	63.6	66.2	65.9	68.4	69.9	69.0	68.6	67.4
0.25 to 2.00 of median	76.4	73.9	76.1	76.3	75.4	74.2	71.3	68.3	68.3	68.4	73.6	72.7	74.0	76.8	74.4	74.2	72.9
Income Shares																	
0.85 to 1.15 of median	14.5	15.2	14.0	13.1	13.2	13.1	12.1	10.4	10.5	11.0	11.0	11.2	11.8	11.9	12.4	11.7	11.5
0.75 to 1.25 of median	23.9	24.5	22.9	21.8	21.9	21.6	20.0	17.5	17.8	18.4	18.2	18.4	19.4	19.7	20.7	19.5	19.1
0.50 to 1.50 of median	45.7	44.9	42.6	42.7	42.4	42.7	39.1	35.2	35.9	36.3	36.4	36.1	37.9	39.6	39.9	38.3	37.5
0.25 to 1.75 of median	63.9	61.1	60.3	60.0	60.2	60.1	55.4	50.5	50.1	48.6	52.1	52.0	55.5	56.0	56.0	53.9	53.4
0.25 to 2.00 of median	72.1	65.8	68.9	71.3	70.4	66.9	61.6	56.6	57.3	56.4	64.0	62.8	64.5	66.8	64.9	62.8	62.1

Source: Statistics Canada, cat. 13-207, various issues; figures have been calculated using an interpolation program designed by the authors (see Beach and Slotsve 1993 for details).

Figure 11: *Middle-Class (Population) Shares for Individual Income Recipients, Canada, 1972–92*
(measured as between 0.5 and 1.5 of median)

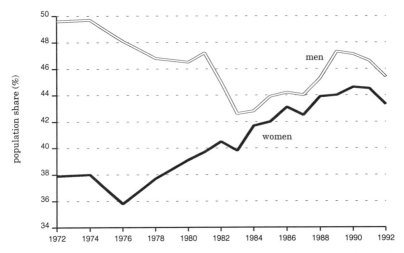

Source: Statistics Canada, cat. 13-207, various issues; figures have been calculated using an interpolation program designed by the authors (see Beach and Slotsve 1993 for details).

share significantly. From 1980 to 1992, the population share of the MC$_{.5}$ measure rose by 11 percent (4.2 percentage points) while the corresponding MC$_{.5}$ income share increased by 15 percent, reflecting a moderate increase in the mean middle-class incomes of women over the period as well.

The middle-class income results for men appear in Table 11. In this case, corresponding to polarization rates for men — which rose and then attenuated over the period — middle-class shares generally declined until 1983–84, and then drifted up until the 1990–92 recession, when they fell again. This pattern is also illustrated in Figure 11 for the MC$_{.5}$ measure. While the middle-class share for men starts off in 1972 at 11.7 percentage points above that of women, it ends up by 1992 only 2.1 percentage points higher. From the regression results in Appendix Table A-4, there is estimated to be no significant trend in the middle-class share for men; once again, it is cyclical factors that drive the results. A decrease in the unemployment rate by 1.0 percentage point and a tightening up of the labor market are estimated to increase significantly the middle-class share for men, by 0.77 of a percentage point (versus an increase of only 0.09 of a percentage point for women). Over the 1980–92 period, the income share for the $MC_{.5}$ measure fell by 12 percent (4.9 percentage points), while the corresponding population share declined by only 2 percent. This pattern implies that mean middle-class incomes for men declined significantly during the 1980s.

Figures for mean real middle-class incomes are presented in Appendix Table A-5 for selected years from 1972 to 1992. Here, three alternative measures of middle-class incomes are used, including the mean of the middle three quintiles of the distribution. The three measures show quite similar patterns. Typically, $MC_{.5}$ turns out to be the lowest of the three values, while the mean of the middle 60 percent provides the highest set of values. Accordingly, these two measures of middle-class mean incomes are graphed in Figures 12 and 13. Mean middle-class incomes for women are substantially lower than those for men. For the $MC_{.5}$ measure, for example, women's middle-class income was only 37.5 percent that of men's in 1980, and this had risen to 54.7 percent by 1992.

The pattern of change for middle-class incomes also differs dramatically between sexes. Women's income clearly increased over the entire period, except for the two severe recessions at the beginning and end of the 1980s. Between 1980 and 1992, mean $MC_{.5}$ incomes for women increased an average of 2.14 percent a year. Men's incomes showed a runup in the mid-1970s and mid-1980s, but experienced marked losses between the peak of 1976 and 1983–84 and again in the 1990–92 recession. Between 1980 and 1992, mean $MC_{.5}$ incomes for men declined an average of 0.72 percent a year. Consequently, middle-class incomes for men in 1992 were indeed less than they were two decades before (in 1971–72). Between 1980 and 1992, women's middle-class incomes (mean $MC_{.5}$) rose by 24 percent, while men's fell by 15 percent.

Figure 12: *Mean Real Incomes of Middle-Class Female Income Recipients, Canada, 1971–92*

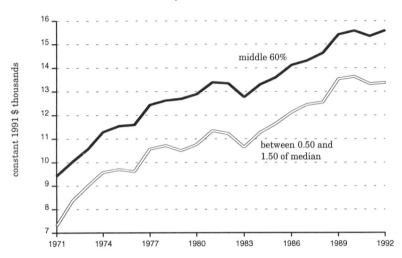

Source:　Statistics Canada, cat. 13-207, various issues; figures have been calculated using an interpolation program designed by the authors (see Beach and Slotsve 1993 for details).

Once again, men's incomes also appear to be more cyclically sensitive than women's. In regressions on mean middle-class incomes similar to those in Appendix Table A-4, the effect of a 1.0 percentage point decline in the unemployment rate is to increase women's mean incomes by 0.22 of a percentage point and raise men's mean incomes by 1.06 percentage points.[8]

By way of summary, women's middle-class population shares all show a distinct upward trend amounting to a 7.3 percentage point increase over the 1972–92 period, with no significant cyclical pattern. Men's middle-class population shares, on the other hand, generally declined from the middle 1970s to 1983–84; they then started moving up again until the later 1980s expansion, when again they fell off. Cyclical factors appear to be the driving forces behind changes in men's middle-class population share,

---

8　With corresponding t-ratios of 2.30 and 7.22, respectively.

Figure 13: *Mean Real Incomes of Middle-Class Male Income Recipients, Canada, 1971–92*

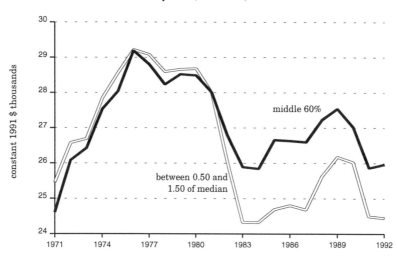

Source: Statistics Canada, cat. 13-207, various issues; figures have been calculated using an interpolation program designed by the authors (see Beach and Slotsve 1993 for details).

with a 1.0 percentage point fall in the unemployment rate estimated to increase their share by 0.77 of a percentage point. Women's middle-class incomes are on average substantially below men's. But while men's fell on average between 1980 and 1992, women's grew quite significantly; their relative middle-class incomes rose from only 37.5 percent of men's in 1980 to 55 percent by 1992.

Chapter 4

Family Incomes and a Declining Middle Class?

While individuals are the recipients of incomes, families or households better represent the unit of shared resources, a common consumption standard, and general economic well-being. When people talk about the polarization of society and a declining middle class, they typically express themselves in terms of families. According to Statistics Canada, an economic family (the concept used in this study) is "a group of individuals related by blood, marriage or adoption who shared a common dwelling unit at the time of the survey" (Statistics Canada, cat. 12-210, 1992, 33). A "family unit" consists either of two or more persons living as a family or of one unattached individual. In this report, we follow Statistics Canada's definition of "families": family units of two or more persons. By this definition a family could be, for example, a married couple with or without children or a lone parent with one or more children.

Polarization of Family Incomes

Alternative polarization measures for family incomes are provided in Table 12. A comparison of these polarization index values with those given for individuals in Tables 7 and 8 shows that family incomes are substantially less polarized than the incomes of individuals. In 1992, for example, 41.1 percent of families had incomes beyond plus or minus 50 percent of the median income for families, while 54.6 percent of individual men and 56.7 per-

Table 12: Alternative Polarization Measures for Family Incomes, Canada, Selected Years 1972–92

	1972	1974	1976	1978	1980	1981	1982	1983	1984	1985	1986	1987	1988	1989	1990	1991	1992
Polarization Indexes (percent)																	
1 (± 50% of median)	38.6	37.2	40.4	40.0	39.4	38.9	40.4	41.7	41.6	41.9	40.4	40.7	40.3	39.7	40.5	40.7	41.1
2 (± 75% of median)	18.0	17.3	18.4	23.7	17.3	19.3	21.5	19.8	19.6	19.2	17.9	18.7	18.4	17.9	18.5	19.2	19.2
Population Shares																	
Below 0.25 of median	5.3	4.6	4.9	4.7	4.8	4.2	4.0	4.5	4.9	4.4	3.9	3.7	3.6	3.4	3.8	3.7	3.9
Below 0.50 of median	18.5	17.2	18.5	18.1	18.6	17.6	18.1	18.3	19.1	18.6	18.0	17.9	17.5	17.2	17.7	17.5	18.0
Above 1.50 of median	20.1	20.1	21.9	21.9	20.8	21.3	22.3	23.4	22.5	23.3	22.4	22.9	22.8	22.5	22.8	23.2	23.1
Above 1.75 of median	12.7	12.8	13.5	19.0	12.6	15.1	17.5	15.2	14.7	14.8	14.0	15.0	14.8	14.5	14.7	15.4	15.3
Above 2.00 of median	8.0	8.9	8.6	16.0	9.5	11.4	13.0	9.7	10.2	11.8	8.7	10.4	11.4	9.3	9.3	10.2	9.7
Income Shares																	
Below 0.25 of median	0.74	0.65	0.71	0.56	0.66	0.59	0.58	0.65	0.73	0.64	0.57	0.54	0.52	0.45	0.51	0.50	0.53
Below 0.50 of median	5.30	4.98	5.31	5.13	5.45	5.26	5.51	5.43	5.71	5.59	5.45	5.47	5.33	5.16	5.29	5.20	5.43
Above 1.50 of median	39.1	38.7	42.3	41.2	39.6	39.9	41.8	44.2	42.9	43.9	42.7	43.2	42.9	42.7	43.1	44.2	43.8
Above 1.75 of median	28.2	27.9	30.2	36.9	27.3	30.8	34.8	32.5	31.5	31.5	30.5	31.9	31.3	31.3	31.4	33.0	32.6
Above 2.00 of median	20.1	21.5	22.0	31.9	22.1	24.4	27.1	23.4	24.2	26.5	21.7	24.3	25.6	22.6	22.4	24.3	23.2

Source: Statistics Canada, cat. 13-207, various issues; figures have been calculated using an interpolation program designed by the authors (see Beach and Slotsve 1993 for details).

cent of individual women had incomes beyond plus or minus 50 percent of the median incomes for individuals of their sex. The fluctuations in polarization of family incomes are also much more damped than those for the incomes of individuals of either sex. It would appear that the pooling of multiple individual incomes to make up family total income has the effect of dampening the degree of polarization and its year-to-year fluctuations.

Looking at the pattern of polarization changes (illustrated in Figure 14), one also notes that, at least in the 1980s, there was surprisingly little change in the polarization indexes compared with the quite strong polarization patterns for individuals. Evidently, marked polarization changes are characteristic of individuals rather than families, where income pooling appears to blunt these effects. One can nonetheless faintly detect the three phases found earlier in the polarization of men's incomes: a bit of an upward trend until about 1984, a slight downward drift over the 1984–89 expansionary period, followed by an upturn with the ensuing recession. However, when the family polarization indexes are regressed on trend and cyclical indicators (see Appendix Table A-6, first column), a slight downward trend is detected, along with an upward cyclical effect from higher unemployment, but neither effect is at all statistically significant. While individuals have experienced significant polarization shifts (up for men and down for women), this does not appear to be the case for families, where the opposing effects have tended to net each other out.

Looking at the lower- and upper-tail population shares separately (see the second panel of Table 12), one notes that the lower shares for family incomes are vastly smaller than those for individual incomes (see Tables 7 and 8). Over the 1980s, for example, the population share of the group of families with incomes below 25 percent of the median ranges between 3.4 percent and 4.9 percent, compared with a range of between 10.4 percent and 13.9 percent for individuals. Either because of compensatory income pooling among income recipients in the household or because of government transfers, the lower end of the family

Figure 14: *Polarization Indexes for Families, Canada, 1972–92*

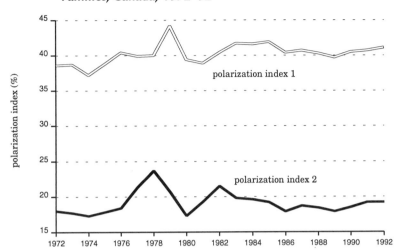

Source: Statistics Canada, cat. 13-207, various issues; figures have been calculated using an interpolation program designed by the authors (see Beach and Slotsve 1993 for details).

income distribution is far closer to the median than is the case for the individual distributions. The upper shares of the family distribution are also somewhat smaller than those for the individual distributions (over the 1980s, the share of the group of families with incomes above 175 percent of the median varied from 12.6 percent to 17.5 percent, compared with ranges of 17.5 percent to 24.6 percent for men and 24.8 percent to 29.2 percent for women). Again, the family tends to homogenize incomes and attenuate polarization. When one looks at the year-to-year variations in population shares, the upper-share fluctuations are generally the more dominant in driving the polarization indexes, particularly in the two major recessions at the beginning and end of the 1980s.

However, the pattern of changes in the lower- and upper-population shares again appears quite different. Regressions on the population shares (see Appendix Table A-6) show that the lower-share fluctuations follow a small but significant downward trend of 0.09 of a percentage point per year (a result that is again consistent with an increasing rate of transfer payments or an increased degree of compensatory income receipts within the family) and a significant cyclical pattern that increases the share of low-income families by 0.16 of a percentage point when unemployment rises by 1.0 percentage point. This combination of a significant negative trend and positive unemployment rate effects on the lower share resembles the pattern found earlier for individual men, but again, the effects are damped somewhat compared with those for men. However, unlike those for either individual group, the upper shares for families show no significant trend or cyclical pattern at all. Since upper-share fluctuations dominate the relatively small lower-share fluctuations, this result accounts for the apparent absence of significant effects for the polarization indexes as a whole. Evidently, other factors are at work at the top end of the family income distribution.

The pattern of income shares (in the lower panel of Table 12) reflects the relative size of the population shares. Family income shares are much smaller than those for individuals, reflecting the much lower population shares at the two ends of the distribution. Over the 1972–92 period as a whole, the lower group's income shares generally trended downward, while upper-income shares drifted up slightly. Between 1972 and 1992, the income share of the group of families with incomes below 25 percent of the median declined by 28.4 percent (0.21 of a percentage point), while that of the group with incomes above 175 percent of the median rose by 15.6 percent (4.4 percentage points). Over the critical recession-and-recovery period of 1981 to 1985, the population share of the group of families with incomes below 25 percent of the median rose by 4.8 percent (0.2 of a percentage point), while the corresponding income share rose by 8.5 percent (0.05 of a percentage point), implying a rise in the relative mean family income of the group. The population share of the group of families with incomes above 175 percent of the median declined by 2.0 percent (0.3 of a percentage point), while its income share rose by 2.3 percent (0.7 of a percentage point), implying a rise in the relative mean income of the upper group as well. Evidently, relative incomes at both ends of the distribution rose over the early 1980s, suggesting that middle-range incomes fell significantly over this period. Over the longer 1980–92 period, the population share for the group of families with incomes below 50 percent of the median fell by 3.2 percent (0.6 of a percentage point), while its income share barely changed, implying that mean incomes for the lower group rose by about 3 percent. For the group of families with incomes above 150 percent of the median, the population share rose by 11.1 percent (2.3 percentage points)between 1980 and 1992, while the income share rose 10.6 percent (4.2 percentage points), imply- ing that mean incomes for the upper group did not rise over the period. Thus, rising income shares for the upper end of the family income distribution seem to be driven primarily by more families' moving up the income scale, from the middle to the upper ranges.

As was the case for individuals, the gains and losses in family incomes are not distributed evenly across families in the economy. As shown in Table 13, income gains are lowest for those families with the youngest and least-educated heads, and highest among those families with heads who are older and those with heads who have the greatest amount of education.[1] The most dramatic differences are between age groups, where families with young heads lost ground over the 1980s compared with families with older or retired heads. These changes follow exactly the same pattern as seen for individuals earlier (in Table 9), but in the case of differences between age groups in the 1980s, differences in family incomes were even more significant. Over the 1980–91 period, the mean real incomes of families with an elderly head aged 70 or over rose by 26.9 percent, while the mean incomes of

---

[1] While the family (as designated by Statistics Canada) head is typically the male spouse if present, the age and education levels of spouses are strongly correlated (0.93 for ages and 0.62 for education levels in 1987 for Canada. See Blackburn and Bloom (1994, table 9).

Table 13:   *Changes in Mean Family Incomes by Age and*
Education of Head, Canada, 1972–91 and 1980–91

	1972–91	1980–91
	(percentage change)	
	Age Group	
20–24	1.0	– 17.6
25–34	12.9	– 5.8
35–44	20.0	0.8
45–54	32.9	9.5
65–69[a]	38.5	24.5
70 and over[a]	58.3	26.9
	Education Group	
0–8 years of education	n.a.	– 7.9
Completed high school	10.3	n.a.
Postsecondary certificate	n.a.	– 2.6
University degree	17.1	9.7

n.a. = not available because of changes in education categories over the period.

[a]   Since mean income figures are not available for these categories for the years 1972 and 1980, the preceding years' figures — that is, those for 1971 and 1979, respectively — are used instead.

Note: Over the 1972–91 period, mean family incomes rose by 24.4 percent; over 1980–91, it rose by 2.6 percent.

Figures could not be readily updated to 1992 because of the published categories of the Statistics Canada data for 1992.

Source: Statistics Canada, cat. 13-207, various issues.

families with the youngest heads (those aged 20 to 24) declined by 17.6 percent. More recent family cohorts have clearly lost out in comparison with their parents' generation, and in the 1980s even slipped markedly in absolute terms. Given that, in the more recent cohorts, family income has been earned by spouses' having spent more time working in the labor market than was the case in the previous generation, the slippage in the economic well-being of the younger cohorts is likely even more marked than these income figures indicate.

In sum, family polarization rates are substantially less than those for individual men or women and exhibit more damped year-to-year fluctuations, reflecting the income-pooling role of families. While upper-income-group population shares tend to dominate year-to-year fluctuations in the family polarization rate, the lower-income-group shares show both a significant downward trend and a significant cyclical effect similar to, though more damped than, that for individual men. The downward trend probably arises from the increasing role of transfers in family incomes, particularly toward the lower end of the distribution, and from an increasing degree of compensatory earnings receipts among spouses within the family. Family income gains in the 1980s also differed widely across households. The most marked differences occurred by age: between 1980 and 1991, the real income of families with young heads (aged 20 to 24) fell by 17.6 percent, while that of families with older heads (aged 65 and over) rose by more than 25 percent. The younger generation of families is not having an easy time in today's labor market.

What Has Happened to the Middle Class and Its Members' Incomes?

The middle class as a social and economic group is conventionally defined with reference to family incomes. Family income provides the resources for a certain standard of living, level of expectations, and status of economic well-being. It also supplies the spending power to support middle-class tastes for goods and services in the economy. A great deal of public concern about economic insecurity, broken expectations, and loss of economic well-being in the 1980s has been expressed in relation to the middle-class experience, particularly when compared with that of previous decades and to the environment of expectations in which many current workers were brought up (in the 1950s and 1960s). What has happened to the middle class since?

Results on the middle-class population shares for families since 1972 are provided in the top panel of Table 14. Compared with the middle-class population shares for individuals (see Tables 10 and 11), the family population shares are much larger. Over the 1980–92 period, the population shares for the families with incomes between 50 percent and 150 percent of the median (the MC.5 measure) ranged between 58.1 and 61.1 percent of all families; the corresponding individual shares are 39.1 percent to 44.6 percent for women and 42.6 percent to 47.3 percent for men. As before, the income-pooling effect of families tends to bring a larger proportion of families toward the middle range of incomes than occurs for individuals.

The year-to-year changes in middle-class population shares generally reflect the converse pattern to that of polarization. If one concentrates on the MC.5 measure, one sees that the middle-class proportion of families peaked in 1974 at 62.8 percent, declined over the later 1970s and early 1980s to trough in 1985 at 58.1 percent, turned around and rose slightly until 1989, and then fell off about a point and a half over the following recessionary years (see Figure 15). The expansionary period following 1985 provides a recovery of only one-quarter of the 1974–85 five-point decline in the middle class population share. Over the decade from 1972 to 1982, the size of the middle class (as measured by MC.5) fell by about 2 percentage points (from 61.4 percent to 59.6 percent of families); then, over the decade from 1982 to 1992, it fell by a further 0.7 of a percentage point (to 58.9 percent of families). The other middle-class measures show a pattern that is generally similar to that of MC.5. All measures but the widest peak in 1974, and all but the widest trough during the 1982–85 period associated with the severe recession at the beginning of the 1980s. By 1991, the second measure (plus or minus 0.25 percent of the median) lies below even its 1985 trough, so that any recovery in the share from the long 1980s' expansion is wiped out by the 1990–92 recession. A regression on the middle-class population shares (see Appendix Table A-6, last column) confirms the significant cyclical effect, which reduces the share in recessionary times and increases it in economic expansions. Each 1.0 percentage point decline in the unemployment rate is estimated to raise

Table 14:   Middle-Class Family Shares, Canada, Selected Years 1972–92

	1972	1974	1976	1978	1980	1981	1982	1983	1984	1985	1986	1987	1988	1989	1990	1991	1992
								(percent)									
Population Shares																	
0.85 to 1.15 of median	22.3	22.3	20.7	21.4	20.6	20.4	19.7	19.0	19.3	19.1	19.5	19.6	19.5	20.3	19.6	19.1	18.7
0.75 to 1.25 of median	35.2	35.8	33.1	34.3	33.2	33.2	32.4	31.3	31.7	31.0	31.9	31.7	32.1	33.0	32.1	30.8	31.0
0.50 to 1.50 of median	61.4	62.8	59.6	60.0	60.6	61.1	59.6	58.3	58.4	58.1	59.6	59.3	59.7	60.3	59.5	59.3	58.9
0.25 to 1.75 of median	82.0	82.7	81.6	76.3	82.7	80.7	78.5	80.2	80.4	80.8	82.1	81.3	81.6	82.1	81.5	80.8	80.8
0.25 to 2.00 of median	86.7	86.5	86.5	79.3	85.7	84.4	83.0	85.8	84.9	83.8	87.4	85.9	85.0	87.3	86.9	86.1	86.4
Income Shares																	
0.85 to 1.15 of median	20.5	20.3	18.4	19.5	19.0	18.6	17.7	16.8	17.4	17.1	17.3	17.4	17.3	17.9	17.5	16.8	16.7
0.75 to 1.25 of median	32.2	32.7	29.4	31.2	30.5	30.3	29.0	27.6	28.4	27.6	28.3	28.0	28.5	29.1	28.4	26.9	27.4
0.50 to 1.50 of median	55.6	56.3	52.4	53.6	55.0	54.9	52.7	50.4	51.4	50.5	51.9	51.3	51.8	52.1	51.6	50.6	50.7
0.25 to 1.75 median	71.1	71.5	69.1	62.6	72.1	68.6	64.6	66.8	67.8	67.9	68.9	67.6	68.2	68.3	68.1	66.5	66.9
0.25 to 2.00 of median	79.1	77.9	77.3	67.6	77.2	75.0	72.3	75.9	75.1	72.9	77.7	75.2	73.9	77.0	77.1	75.1	76.2
Middle 20%	18.4	18.2	17.9	18.3	18.4	18.3	18.1	17.8	18.0	18.0	17.8	17.8	18.0	17.7	17.9	17.6	17.8
Middle 40%	36.7	36.4	35.9	36.7	36.8	36.8	36.3	35.8	36.1	36.1	35.8	35.8	36.0	35.7	35.9	35.5	35.7
Middle 60%	55.1	54.9	54.2	55.6	55.5	55.5	55.0	54.2	54.5	54.6	54.2	54.2	54.6	54.1	54.3	53.8	54.1
Middle 80%	74.4	74.4	73.4	77.2	74.9	76.0	76.1	73.8	74.2	74.7	73.6	74.0	74.6	73.7	74.0	73.6	73.9

Source: Statistics Canada, cat. 13-207, various issues; figures have been calculated using an interpolation program designed by the authors (see Beach and Slotsve 1993 for details).

Figure 15: *Middle-Class Population and*
                Income Shares for Families, Canada, 1972–92
                (measured as between 0.5 and 1.5 of median)

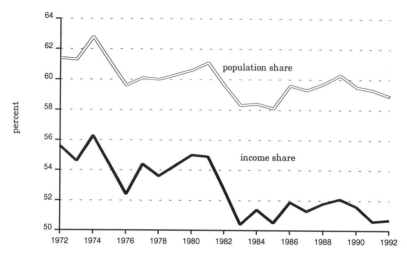

Source: Statistics Canada, cat. 13-207, various issues; figures have been calculated using
          an interpolation program designed by the authors (see Beach and Slotsve 1993
          for details).

the proportion of families in the middle class by about one-third
(0.35) of a percentage point. we found no statistically significant
trend over the 1972–92 period as a whole. That is, the size of the
middle class does not seem to have decreased over the past two
decades once cyclical factors are taken into account. The driving
force behind the declining share of the middle class appears to be
predominantly cyclical. If the unemployment rate can be brought
down, the middle class will increase significantly. Cutting the
unemployment rate from 11 to 5 percent would, we estimate,
raise the size of the middle class (as measured by $MC_{.5}$) by more
than 2 percentage points.

   While population shares indicate the size of the middle class,
income shares and means indicate how well members of this
group have done. The median-based income shares in Table 14

show generally the same pattern as the population shares. The income share for the $MC_{.5}$ measure peaked in 1974, declined thereafter to trough in the 1983–85 period, then rose slightly until 1989, after which it subsided again (see also Figure 15). According to the $MC_{.5}$ measure, by 1992, the 58.9 percent of families that constituted the middle class received 50.7 percent of all family income. While the population share of the middle-class $MC_{.5}$ group fell by 2.5 percentage points (4.1 percent) between 1972 and 1992, the same group's income share fell by about twice as much (4.9 percentage points or 8.8 percent). Thus, mean middle-class incomes over this 20-year period fell by 4.7 percent compared with mean family incomes as a whole. Middle-class incomes rose more slowly than family incomes as a whole between 1972 and 1992.

Since middle-class income shares have also been expressed in terms of middle-quintile income shares (typically the middle 60 percent of families), several quintile-based income-share measures are also reported in Table 14. They show relatively less year-to-year variation compared with the median-based measures. Moreover, they all peak in 1977 (for example, at a value of 56.0 percent for the middle-three-quintile measure) and generally drift down throughout the 1980s to trough in 1991 (at 53.8 percent for the latter measure).

Mean income figures for middle-class families are presented in Appendix Table A-7 and illustrated in Figure 16. Again, three alternative measures are provided, all of which show a similar pattern of markedly slower growth of incomes in the 1980s than in the 1970s. In the case of the $MC_{.5}$ measure, middle-class mean incomes grew at an average annual rate of 2.07 percent between 1972 and 1980, but at a rate of only 0.36 percent per year between 1980 and 1992. All three income series grew through the 1970s, peaking in 1979 or 1980, before the early 1980s' recession reduced middle-class incomes by 7 to 8 percent. They again moved up in the mid-1980s, peaking in 1989, and then declining in the 1990–92 recession.

Figure 16: *Mean Real Incomes of*
**   *Middle-Class Families, Canada, 1971–92***

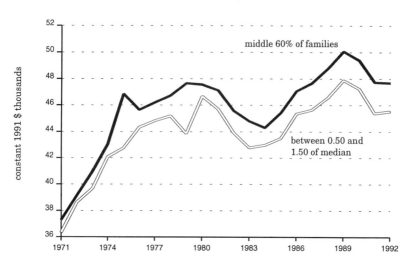

Source: Statistics Canada, cat. 13-207, various issues; figures have been calculated using
          an interpolation program designed by the authors (see Beach and Slotsve 1993
          for details).

Regressions on middle-class incomes (shown in Appendix
Table A-8, using the MC.5 measure) show that, controlling for
cyclical factors, mean middle-class income trended upward by
1.1 percent a year over the 1972–92 period. Again, cyclical factors
are important: a 6.0 percentage point fall in the unemployment
rate is estimated to increase middle-class incomes by 10.5 percent. These trend and cyclical effects are virtually the same as for
median family income as a whole. Mean family income over the
period is estimated to have a slightly higher trend rate (at
1.3 percent a year) and slightly lower cyclical sensitivity.

    In summary, by the beginning of the 1990s, the middle class
was smaller than it had been in the mid-1970s, and the mean
middle-class income had barely changed from what it had been
in the late 1970s. Over the 1972–92 period as a whole, the size of
the middle class declined slightly (by about 4 percent using one
convenient measure). The most marked declines in the size of the

middle class, though, occurred over the decade 1974–85; since then, the decline of the middle class has fluctuated somewhat less. Indeed, no significant downward trend is found once the effect of cyclical factors is netted out. The principal determining factor of these changes appears not to be a long-run trend, but the unemployment rate, which indicates the general health of the labor market.

Chapter 5

The Rising Tax Burden and Economic Insecurity in the 1980s

Average Canadian incomes grew far more slowly in the 1980s than in the 1970s and earlier decades. The concern and frustration expressed in the popular media focus on the increased tax burden borne by individual workers and families: personal taxes rose faster in Canada in the later 1980s than in any other member country of the Organisation for Economic Co-operation and Development (Cook 1994). Public concern in Canada and the United States has also highlighted the more rapid turnover in labor markets as new jobs replace older ones at a faster pace and major employers continue to downsize their work force, with the result that workers feel increased insecurity and vulnerability about potential job loss and its consequences (Canadian Council on Social Development 1993; Uchitelle 1994). We now turn to these concerns.

If real incomes for many have stalled (or even declined), increased taxes mean reduced disposable income. If disposable household income does not improve and if, due to a continuing sense of economic insecurity, consumer confidence does not rise, household consumption expenditures will be slow to move up, and Canada's current, still-tentative expansion will be less robust and shorter lived than is desirable. Even those with significantly higher incomes (such as women earners) on average move into higher tax brackets; moreover, their higher incomes are earned by increased average hours worked in the labor market. Also, to what extent have higher taxes been distributed across the population, particularly on the middle class? Have taxes accentuated or dampened the polarization results already found? These questions are addressed in the next section.

In previous chapters, we looked only at pre-tax income. In this chapter, we examine income taxes and post-tax income, and Canada's current expansion. The concept of taxes used in this study is essentially the income tax definition of Statistics Canada: income after tax is total money income (defined in Chapter 3, under the subheading "Data, Concepts, and Methodology") less income tax payable, and

> income tax payable...is the sum of federal and provincial income taxes payable on...income and capital gains. Provincial tax credits, the child tax credit, the goods and services tax credit, and the federal sales tax credit have not been deducted from income tax payable. (Statistics Canada 1992, 34.)

Essentially, taxes here refer just to personal income taxes, and after-tax income is what remains after personal income taxes are deducted. The available data do not take account of social security contributions (such as payroll taxes for unemployment insurance or the Canada and Quebec Pension Plans) or the goods and services tax (and its predecessor, the manufacturers' sales tax) or provincial sales taxes. The after-tax analysis of this report thus incorporates about half the total tax burden on the population (Cook 1994, 8). The distribution of the effective burden on the various nonpersonal taxes is, however, beyond the scope of this study; moreover, it is under considerable debate in the discipline. We restrict our analysis to the distribution data that are available. Consequently, the tax rates and tax burden discussed in the next section essentially refer to personal (federal and provincial) income taxes.

A strong sense of economic insecurity about labor market change has recently been highlighted in the media:

> [A] changing economy is gradually linking highly educated managers and technicians with high-school-trained assem-

bly-line workers and office clerks. The link is in their common place in an increasingly competitive economy....What they share, public opinion polls show, are feelings of uncertainty, insecurity and anxiety about their jobs and their incomes....

"For the first time in 50 years, we are recording a decline in people's expectations," [says] Richard T. Curtin, director of the University of Michigan's Consumer Surveys. "And their uncertainty and anxiety grow the farther you ask them to look into the future." (Uchitelle 1994, 4.1, 4.3.)[1]

Is this true for Canada? As far as we know, a formal analysis of economic insecurity has not heretofore been undertaken. Consequently, the second section of this chapter, "Distributional Estimates of Economic Insecurity," takes a first step in this direction. Economic insecurity is viewed in terms of the probability of falling out of the middle class and the expected income losses should this occur. Expressed in these terms, economic insecurity indexes can be constructed from the results already obtained in this study. Such indexes serve to integrate the study's results into a general framework and help to identify the factors driving these concerns.

The Rising Tax Burden of the 1980s

The rising tax burden on families is clearly evident from the figures in Table 15. In 1992, the median family after-tax income was $38,945 (in 1991 dollars), while the mean was $42,716. The tax burden rose from 13.3 percent of median family income in 1971 to a 1991 peak of 17.6 percent. Almost all of the 4.5 percentage point rise in the average tax rate between 1971 and 1991 occurred in the 1980s. The average rate of growth in median after-tax family income was 2.51 percent per year from 1971 to 1980 and 0.05 percent per year — basically no growth at all — from 1980 to 1992. These growth rates compare with the corre-

---

1 See also Burtless (1990); Danziger and Gottschalk (1993); Levy and Michel (1991); Manegold (1994); Phillips (1993).

Table 15: *After-Tax Income and Tax Burden*
of Families, Canada, 1971–92

	Mean After-Tax Income	Tax Burden	Median After-Tax Income	Tax Burden
	(constant 1991 $)	*(%)*	*(constant 1991 $)*	*(%)*
1971	34,747	15.3	32,053	13.3
1972	36,084	15.5	33,640	14.1
1973	37,758	15.3	35,012	13.4
1974	39,777	15.2	37,045	13.3
1975	40,358	14.9	37,528	12.8
1976	42,419	16.0	38,831	13.8
1977	42,212	14.6	39,656	12.9
1978	43,206	14.6	40,119	13.2
1979	42,523	15.2	39,653	14.1
1980	43,466	16.1	40,317	15.8
1981	43,037	15.4	39,901	14.2
1982	42,006	15.5	38,485	14.1
1983	41,620	16.0	38,061	13.6
1984	41,085	15.9	37,811	13.9
1985	42,624	14.8	38,936	13.1
1986	42,966	17.4	39,122	15.9
1987	42,919	18.6	39,035	16.9
1988	43,731	18.5	39,946	16.6
1989	44,766	19.3	40,678	17.4
1990	43,757	19.8	40,068	17.6
1991	42,612	19.8	38,535	17.6
1992	42,716	19.2	38,945	17.3

Sources: After-tax incomes are from Statistics Canada, cat. 13-210, various issues;
before-tax incomes are from Statistics Canada, cat. 13-207, various issues.
Current incomes have been converted to constant 1991 dollars by the authors
(based on the consumer price index).

Figure 17: *Mean and Median Real After-Tax Family Incomes, Canada, 1971–92*

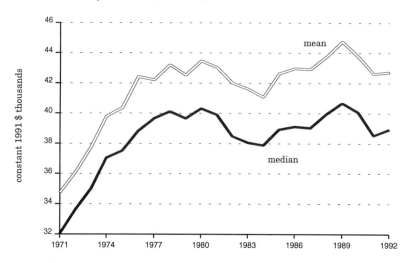

Sources: Statistics Canada, cat. 13-210, various issues; and authors' calculations (the conversion of current incomes to constant 1991 dollars, based on the consumer price index).

sponding growth rates of 2.65 percent per year and 0.44 percent per year for median total income before taxes from the figures in Table 2. The larger tax bite has flattened any growth that occurred in family incomes in the 1980s. This situation is also apparent in Figure 17, which shows that after-tax incomes in 1992 were essentially where they were 15 years earlier, in 1976 (when median after-tax income was $38,831 in 1991 dollars). Not surprisingly, growth in disposable income and, hence, household consumption expenditures has not been driving the current expansion.

Corresponding mean after-tax incomes and average tax rates for individual men and women are listed in Appendix Table A-9; the mean after-tax incomes are illustrated in Figure 18. While the mean after-tax income for women rose fairly steadily over the period, men's mean after-tax income declined fairly steadily from its peak in 1976. Both curves in Figure 18 show reduced growth

Figure 18: *Mean After-Tax Real Incomes of Men and Women, Canada, 1971–92*

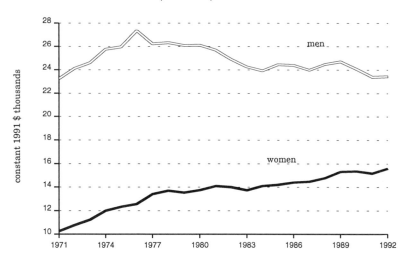

Sources: Statistics Canada, cat. 13-210, various issues; and authors' calculations (the conversion of current incomes to constant 1991 dollars, based on the consumer price index).

compared with the mean pre-tax income curves for the 1980s[2] in Figure 5. While the average rate of growth of women's median after-tax income declined from 3.97 percent per year between 1971 and 1980 to a rate of 1.44 percent per year between 1980 and 1992, the corresponding average growth rates for men were 1.28 percent per year in the 1970s and − 0.78 percent per year in the 1980s. Indeed, men's after-tax income for 1992 was on a par with what it was more than two decades previously, in 1971 ($23,451 in 1992 versus $23,250 in 1971 — again in 1991 dollars).

Average tax rates also vary by income class. Table 16 shows average effective tax rates by quintile group for family income. As is to be expected with a progressive income tax, higher quintile groups pay higher tax rates. In 1992, for example, the average

2 The increased tax bite for women in the 1980s was felt even more due to the apparent reduction in effective tax rates for women over the first half of the 1970s.

Table 16:   *Effective Average Family Income Tax Rates*
              by Quintile, Canada, 1971–92

	Bottom Quintile	Second Quintile	Third Quintile	Fourth Quintile	Top Quintile	Total
	(percent)					
1971	2.4	8.9	13.0	15.1	20.2	15.3
1972	2.4	9.2	13.4	15.7	20.3	15.5
1976	2.6	9.4	13.4	16.1	20.8	15.9
1980	2.7	9.8	14.0	16.2	19.6	15.4
1981	2.7	9.7	13.8	16.4	19.6	15.4
1982	2.1	8.9	13.6	16.5	20.3	15.6
1983	2.1	8.9	13.9	16.8	20.8	16.0
1984	1.6	8.6	13.7	16.6	21.0	15.9
1985	2.3	9.4	14.3	17.3	21.3	16.4
1986	2.9	10.9	15.6	18.3	22.2	17.4
1987	3.3	11.7	16.5	19.7	23.5	18.6
1988	3.0	11.1	16.4	19.6	23.8	18.5
1989	3.7	12.2	17.1	19.9	24.7	19.3
1990	3.4	12.1	17.4	20.5	25.4	19.8
1991	3.4	11.6	17.2	20.6	25.6	19.8
1992	3.0	10.7	16.5	20.0	25.2	19.2
	(percentage change)					
1971–91	42%	30%	32%	36%	27%	29%
1980–91	26%	18%	23%	27%	31%	29%
1971–92	25%	20%	27%	32%	25%	25%
1980–92	11%	9%	18%	23%	29%	25%

Source: Statistics Canada, cat. 13-210, 1994, 38–39.

tax rate for the bottom quintile was 3.0 percent, while for the top quintile of families it was 25.2 percent. The average tax rate overall (shown in the right-hand column) is above the middle quintile's rate because of the large amount of taxes paid by the upper quintile groups. As the bottom rows of the table show, the increases in effective tax rates in the 1980s were not borne

Table 17:   *Gini Coefficients for Different Concepts of*
            Family Income, Canada, Selected Years 1971–92

	Income before Transfers (1)	Total Money Income (2)	Ratio % (2)/(1) (3)	Income after Tax (4)	Ratio % (4)/(2) (5)
1971	.386	.343	88.9	.313	91.3
1972	.377	.331	87.9	.301	90.9
1976	.394	.340	86.4	.310	91.1
1980	.372	.319	85.8	.293	91.8
1981	.372	.318	85.5	.291	91.5
1982	.392	.326	83.2	.296	90.8
1983	.404	.334	82.7	.302	90.4
1984	.407	.334	82.1	.302	90.4
1985	.401	.330	82.3	.299	90.6
1986	.402	.331	82.3	.299	90.3
1987	.401	.330	82.3	.296	89.7
1988	.399	.328	82.2	.291	88.7
1989	.395	.328	83.0	.292	89.0
1990	.403	.331	82.1	.292	88.2
1991	.420	.337	80.2	.297	88.1
1992	.425	.336	79.1	.295	87.8

Source: Statistics Canada, cat. 13-210, 1994, 42.

evenly across the distribution. The largest increase occurred for high- income families, while the smallest occurred in the second quintile.[3] Between 1980 and 1992, for example, the average tax rate in the top quintile rose by 29 percent, while in the second quintile it rose by only 9 percent.

The increased equalizing effect of the progressive income tax is shown in Table 17 in terms of Gini coefficients for family

---

3 This pattern contrasts with that seen in the 1970s, when the effective tax rate of the top quintile declined slightly.

income. The table's first two columns show the effect of transfers on income inequality. Transfers here include income from such government support programs as income assistance, unemployment insurance, workers' compensation, the Canada and Quebec Pension Plans, and the former family allowances. While income before transfers (principally labor market income) has generally increased in inequality since 1971 (see also the lower panel of Table 1), inequality after transfers (that is, total family income) has declined slightly. Between 1980 and 1992, inequality in market incomes rose by 14.3 percent (as measured by the Gini coefficient), but when transfers are added in, inequality in total income increased by only 5.3 percent. Transfers thus largely compensated for rising inequality in market incomes during the 1980s. The effect of income taxes has also been to reduce inequality quite substantially. As indicated in the table's last column, the size of the reduction in inequality increased quite markedly in the 1980s as the upper-income groups saw their taxes rise relatively more. Greater detail on after-tax incomes broken down by decile group is presented in Appendix Table A-10 for selected years. Clearly evident are the higher after-tax income shares (compare these figures with those shown in Table 4 for total family income) for the lower-decile groups and the reduced after-tax shares for the upper-decile groups — again consistent with the idea that income taxes have an inequality-reducing effect.

What has happened to the after-tax incomes of the middle class? Mean after-tax incomes for middle-class families (using our three alternative measures) are listed in Table 18. The higher and lower measures are illustrated in Figure 19; they can be seen to follow each other fairly closely. The average rate of growth of the $MC_{.5}$ measure of middle-class mean after-tax family incomes was 2.37 percent a year over the 1971–80 period;[4] subsequently, growth declined by an average of 0.01 percent a year over the 1980–92

---

4 The corresponding average growth rates, if estimated starting with 1972 rather than 1971, are 2.06 percent per year for the $MC_{.5}$ measure and 2.26 percent per year for the middle three quintiles.

Table 18:   *Mean After-Tax Incomes of*
Middle-Class Families, Canada, 1972–92

	Between 0.75 and 1.25 of Median	Between 0.50 and 1.50 of Median	Middle 60% of Families
	(constant 1991 $)		
1972	33,501	32,992	33,812
1973	34,702	34,496	35,486
1974	37,086	36,158	37,272
1975	37,022	37,108	38,031
1976	38,643	38,201	39,206
1977	39,345	39,111	40,121
1978	39,882	39,035	40,574
1979	39,401	38,162	40,354
1980	40,053	39,583	40,735
1981	39,755	38,912	40,309
1982	38,149	36,749	39,193
1983	37,723	36,916	38,589
1984	37,719	36,783	38,117
1985	38,699	37,837	39,403
1986	38,825	37,901	39,609
1987	38,728	37,624	39,543
1988	39,614	38,638	40,449
1989	40,247	39,542	41,322
1990	39,693	38,738	40,672
1991	38,121	37,191	39,212
1992	38,639	37,610	39,503

Source: Statistics Canada, cat. 13-210, various issues; figures have been calculated using an interpolation program designed by the authors (see Beach and Slotsve 1993 for details).

Figure 19: *Mean After-Tax Real Incomes of*
Middle-Class Families, Canada, 1971–92

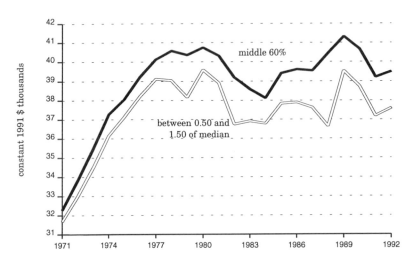

Source: Statistics Canada, cat. 13-207, various issues; figures have been calculated using
          an interpolation program designed by the authors (see Beach and Slotsve 1993
          for details).

period — that is, no growth occurred in middle-class after-tax
family incomes during the 1980s up to 1992. Corresponding
figures for the middle 60 percent of incomes were 2.58 percent
per year and 0.08 percent per year, respectively. These rates are
essentially no different from those for median after-tax income
for all families over the periods in question. Middle-class after-tax
family incomes for 1992 were at approximately the level they
were at in 1975–76. Men's middle-class after-tax incomes (within
plus or minus 50 percent of the median) rose by an average of
0.95 percent a year between 1971 and 1980, and then declined by
an average of 0.86 percent a year from 1980 to 1992. Women's
middle-class after-tax incomes grew at rates of 4.04 percent a year
and 1.45 percent a year, respectively, during the 1970s and 1980s.

By comparing the mean after-tax family income figures in
Table 18 with those for mean total family income (see Appendix
Table A-7), one can work out effective tax rates for middle-class

Table 19:   *Effective Tax Rates for Middle-Class Families, Canada, Selected Years 1972–92*

	Between 0.75 and 1.25 of Median	Between 0.50 and 1.50 of Median	Middle 60% of Families
	(percent)		
1972	14.4	14.6	13.6
1980	15.3	15.2	14.3
1991	18.0	18.1	17.9
1992	17.5	17.4	17.2

Sources: Table 18 and Appendix Table A-7.

families between 1972 and 1992; these are shown for selected years in Table 19.

These middle-class tax rates are all below the average family tax rates shown in Table 16, though slightly above those for the middle quintile of the family income distribution. While the average effective tax rate increased by 28.6 percent during the 1980s (between 1980 and 1991), the corresponding increases in the middle-class tax rate were only 17.6 percent, 19.1 percent, and 25.2 percent, respectively, for the three measures in Table 18. That is, the income tax burden on the middle class increased less in the 1980s than did the average tax rate for all Canadian families. The reason for this is that the average tax rate for upper- and middle-upper-income families increased markedly more over the period, thereby pulling up the average tax burden across all families. While the middle-class tax burden did indeed increase substantially during the 1980s, it rose proportionally less than did the tax burden for the upper portions of the distribution.

In summary, average income tax burdens rose substantially in the 1980s — by close to 29 percent between 1980–81 and 1991–92. Median family after-tax income essentially did not grow at all in the 1980s; in 1992, it was virtually the same as it had been 16 years earlier, in 1976. The increase in the personal tax

burden between 1980 and 1992 varied across the income distribution, from a 9 percent increase for the second quintile of families to a 29 percent increase for the top quintile. Progressivity of
the income tax reduced income inequality substantially over this
period, by about 40 percent to 50 percent of the corresponding
inequality-reducing effect of government transfers. The effective
income tax burden on the middle class for the period is below the
average family tax rate by 1 to 2 percentage points, and increased
less in the 1980s than did the average tax rate for families as a
whole or that for upper-income families in particular.

Distributional Estimates of Economic Insecurity in the 1980s

The concept of economic insecurity is not well defined. It could
refer to an increased likelihood of downward economic mobility.
As discussed in past reports and public opinion surveys, though,
it appears especially to involve concern about losing one's job and
living on a reduced income for an indefinite period. This risk can
be viewed as having two dimensions: the likelihood of exposure
to a fall in income, and the expected income drop that could occur
given a loss of income. These ideas could be readily articulated in
a formal discussion of income expectations in a dynamic labor
market. However, in this study we restrict our attention to the
grouped income data already available, in the absence of readily
available Canadian data on individuals through time over the
period of the study. The grouped data of this report also capture only net flow changes between income groups and not the
more informative gross flow patterns that would show how many
people actually move up or down the distribution from one year
to the next or over the longer term.

Economic insecurity could also be expressed in terms of job
turnover statistics or unemployment rates and durations of unemployment spells. But published data on such statistics are not
expressed in terms of a distributional dimension — and, again,

actual individual survey data (which would be needed for such a study) are not readily available to researchers in Canada. We would also argue, though, that, while the original source of insecurity worries lies in labor market activity, the ultimate concern of workers and families is about loss of income and the potential loss of economic and social status, consumption standard, and general economic well-being. For these reasons, we examine the concept of economic insecurity in terms of incomes rather than employment and jobs.

The two dimensions of (a) expected *incidence* of income loss and (b) an expected *income gap* conditional on a loss of income yield two alternative sets of economic insecurity indexes. These two dimensions can be viewed as analogous to two dimensions commonly found in the literature on poverty in the economy: the incidence of poverty (that is, the proportion of a population, such as single parents or the elderly, who are poor by some measure) and the so-called poverty gap (that is, the proportional amount by which average incomes among the poor fall below some designated low-income cutoff or poverty line).[5]

The first set of economic insecurity indexes reflects the incidence of significant income loss. By this is meant the probability or likelihood that an individual's (or family's) income could fall into some lower-income range, such as below 50 percent of the median of a distribution. The index is calculated as the proportion of the population in a distribution in some lower-income group divided by the proportion of the population in the middle-income group or below. If the occurrence of major job loss in the middle and lower regions of the distribution is indeed purely random, this index represents the probability of landing in the lower-income region from such an event. Where the lower-income group is measured as below 50 percent of the median and the middle-income group is within 50 percent of the median (the

---

5 For illustrations of these two measures, see, for example, National Council of Welfare (1994) and Statistics Canada, cat. 13-207 (1993).

MC.5 measure), the economic insecurity index is calculated as follows:

$$\frac{\textit{Population share below } 0.5 \textit{ of median}}{\textit{Population share below } 1.5 \textit{ of median}}.$$

Again, this measure is interpreted as representing the probability that a random individual (or family) from the middle class or below could be "polarized" into the lower-income group. It thus captures the polarization aspect of economic insecurity, since it is based on relative population shares toward the bottom end of the distribution. We call this index the *random incidence measure*.

The second set of indexes reflects the expected income loss that could occur from a fall from the middle class into the lower-income group for a person at random who experienced such a major job loss. Measuring the lower- and middle-income groups as we did above, this index would be calculated as follows:

$$\frac{\textit{Mean income within } 0.5 \textit{ of median} - \textit{mean income below } 0.5 \textit{ of median}}{\textit{Mean income within } 0.5 \textit{ of median}}.$$

This proportional mean income gap can be viewed as capturing the inequality aspect of economic insecurity, since it is based on relative income differentials. We call this index the *income gap measure*.

Additionally, one could combine the two measures. If the first represents an incidence of a loss and the second the expected size of an associated income loss, multiplying the two together can be interpreted as indicating the probability-weighted expected income loss. This composite measure is referred to as the *weighted proportional mean income gap*.[6] It can be viewed as incorporating both the polarization and the income inequality aspects of economic insecurity.

---

6   It can be shown that this third index is equal to the ratio of population shares of lower group to middle-class group minus the ratio of income shares of lower group to middle-class group.

Each of these alternative indexes can be implemented with the different measures of lower- and middle-income groups used in this study. Rather than attempt to be exhaustive, we have selected the measures that seem to be most frequently cited in the literature. For the lower-income group, we use those below 75 percent of the median, below 50 percent of the median, and below 25 percent of the median. For the middle-income group, we focus on the $MC_{.5}$ measure (those within 50 percent of the median). For quintile measures, we use the lowest quintile (20 percent) or decile (10 percent) compared to the middle 60 percent of the distribution. These alternative measures for estimating economic insecurity are displayed in Table 20.[7]

Turning to the results in Table 20 for families, one notices that the incidence and gap measures highlight different aspects of economic insecurity. In 1992, the random incidence of being in the lower-income group was 44.4 percent for the most broadly defined lower-income group and only 5.1 percent for the narrowest bottom-income group. The incidence or relative population shares show a peak just after the major recession early in the 1980s and again following the 1990–92 recession. More specifically, the incidence of smaller but substantial income losses (see the first row) peaks in 1984 or 1985, while that of the most catastrophic losses (see the third row) is highest in the earliest year covered (1972). That is, the random incidence of substantial declines in income (the first row) increased from the middle 1970s until 1985; thereafter, it attenuated partially with the expansion in the later 1980s until the recent recession, when it moved up again, reaching a new peak in 1992. The incidence of catastrophic income losses, in contrast, decreased throughout until the upturn in the recent recession. This probability seems to be driven less by cyclical factors than by a decreasing underlying long-run

---

7 One notes that the population share measures in the top panel of Table 20 have no quintile-based measures. This is because quintile or decile population shares, by definition, are always 20 percent or 10 percent, respectively, of the population; hence, the ratio of such shares never varies.

Table 20: *Alternative Indexes of Economic Insecurity for Families, Canada, Selected Years 1972–92*

	1972	1974	1976	1978	1980	1981	1982	1983	1984	1985	1986	1987	1988	1989	1990	1991	1992
							(percent)										
Population Shares																	
Below 0.75 of median/ below 1.50 of median	.408	.401	.419	.416	.422	.419	.424	.437	.438	.443	.431	.434	.430	.421	.432	.442	.444
Below 0.50 of median/ below 1.50 of median	.231	.215	.237	.232	.234	.224	.232	.238	.247	.242	.233	.232	.227	.222	.229	.228	.234
Below 0.25 of median/ below 1.50 of median	.066	.057	.062	.060	.060	.053	.052	.059	.063	.058	.051	.048	.047	.044	.050	.049	.051
Proportional Mean Income Gap																	
Below 0.75 median gap/ within 50% of median	.543	.529	.538	.537	.535	.523	.522	.520	.530	.519	.517	.511	.510	.511	.513	.507	.510
Below 0.50 median gap/ within 50% of median	.683	.677	.672	.682	.676	.668	.655	.656	.660	.654	.653	.647	.649	.652	.654	.652	.649
Below 0.25 median gap/ within 50% of median	.845	.842	.833	.867	.847	.842	.836	.834	.832	.833	.835	.833	.835	.846	.847	.844	.842
Bottom-quintile gap/ middle 60%	.671	.654	.668	.673	.668	.654	.650	.656	.663	.656	.649	.644	.642	.641	.648	.646	.647
Bottom-decile gap/ middle 60%	.777	.762	.767	.783	.770	.757	.748	.755	.762	.753	.745	.740	.739	.739	.748	.745	.747
Weighted Proportional Mean Income Gap																	
Below 0.75 median gap/ within 50% of median	.222	.212	.225	.223	.226	.219	.221	.227	.232	.230	.223	.222	.219	.215	.222	.224	.226
Below 0.50 median gap/ within 50% of median	.158	.146	.159	.158	.158	.150	.152	.156	.163	.158	.152	.150	.147	.145	.150	.149	.152
Below 0.25 median gap/ within 50% of median	.056	.048	.052	.052	.051	.045	.044	.049	.052	.048	.043	.040	.039	.037	.042	.041	.043
Bottom-quintile gap/ middle 60%	.168	.164	.167	.168	.167	.164	.163	.164	.166	.164	.162	.161	.161	.160	.162	.162	.162
Bottom-decile gap/ middle 60%	.097	.095	.096	.098	.096	.095	.094	.094	.095	.094	.093	.093	.092	.092	.094	.093	.093

Source: Statistics Canada, cat. 13-207, various issues; figures have been calculated using an interpolation program designed by the authors (see Beach and Slotsve 1993 for details).

trend. That is, the random incidence of moderate or substantial income losses has indeed generally increased since the 1970s, with the most rapid increases occurring between the mid-1970s and mid-1980s; by 1992, it had returned to another peak with the recent lengthy recession, whereas the random incidence of catastrophic income losses had become considerably smaller by the later 1980s than it had been in the early 1970s. While the random incidence of moderate or substantial income losses was just as high following the late 1980s' recession as for the early 1980s' recession, that of catastrophic income losses was markedly less.

The income gap measures all show a general downward drift from the 1970s until the mid- to late 1980s. The expected relative mean income gap between middle-class and lower-income families in 1992 was 51 percent of middle-class mean incomes (for the widest lower-income group). The narrowest measure decreases right through to 1991, while the widest measure troughed earlier, in the mid-1980s. Again, a long-run trend seems to be shifting these measures of economic insecurity down in the 1980s compared with their generally higher values in the 1970s. The weighted income gap measures in the table's bottom panel tell much the same story as the unweighted income gap measures in its middle panel. The first two measures in the bottom panel, though, also show a strong incidence effect: each troughs in 1974 and generally rises until the 1984 peak. Again, the rise of the random incidence aspect of a substantial, though not catastrophic, income fall appears important over the 1974–85 period.

Overall, however, a general downward trend persists in the income gap and composite measures of economic insecurity in family income. Several factors could contribute to this downward trend. The increase in multiple-earner families over the period (from an average of 1.58 earners per family in 1972 to 1.80 in 1989 and back to 1.70 in 1992 (see Statistics Canada, cat. 13-207, 1993, 19) reduces the dependence of family income on the earnings of a sole breadwinner, so that, when a loss occurs, its effect is buffered by an ongoing second — and even third — income in the household.[8] Earnings as a component of total family income also declined steadily over the period — from 88 percent of family income in 1971 to 78 percent by 1992. Any fall in a declining component of total income will again have a diluted effect. As already pointed out, the role of government transfers, especially toward the lower end of the distribution, increased dramatically over the period. In 1971, transfers constituted 6 percent of family income; by 1992, this fraction had more than doubled, to 13 percent (see Statistics Canada, cat. 13-207, selected years, table 22) — again tempering the effect of earnings losses, particularly through increases in unemployment insurance, social assistance, Canada and Quebec Pension Plan receipts, and workers' compensation payouts.

While in the public's mind economic insecurity may most likely be associated with actual income receipts rather than with after-tax income, it may be worth examining similar results for the above indexes on family after-tax income. Such an examination would indicate the net effect after income taxes of the incidence of expected income losses. These results are presented in Table 21, which is constructed analogously to the previous table. As one would expect, the after-tax economic insecurity figures are generally less than the before-tax figures. A progressive income tax attenuates income losses and reduces the size of expected net income losses. Note also that the major patterns of change found in Table 20 also come through in Table 21, though in some respects slightly modified. The random incidence of noncatastrophic income losses (see the top panel's first row) and the corresponding composite index (see the bottom panel's first row) again show a rise between 1974 and 1984. The remaining measures, however, are dominated by the general downward shift in the insecurity indexes — for all the reasons already mentioned

---

8 The increased number of earners in a family arises not only from the increased labor force participation of married women, but also from the 1980s' increase in the number of adult children who, in the face of a hostile labor market and falling real earnings, moved back into their parents' household.

Table 21: Alternative After-Tax Indexes of Economic Insecurity for Families, Canada, Selected Years 1972–92

	1972	1974	1976	1978	1980	1981	1982	1983	1984	1985	1986	1987	1988	1989	1990	1991	1992
(percent)																	
Population Share Ratio																	
Below 0.75 of median/below 1.50 of median	.379	.377	.386	.378	.383	.383	.395	.393	.397	.391	.390	.388	.382	.375	.385	.388	.387
Below 0.50 of median/below 1.50 of median	.194	.187	.199	.195	.192	.182	.181	.183	.188	.177	.172	.165	.166	.165	.166	.164	.162
Below 0.25 of median/below 1.50 of median	.049	.044	.045	.046	.043	.040	.038	.044	.046	.040	.037	.035	.033	.027	.031	.030	.029
Proportional Mean Income Gap																	
Below 0.75 median gap/within 50% of median	.516	.505	.515	.510	.511	.496	.480	.492	.497	.488	.481	.475	.476	.475	.474	.470	.473
Below 0.50 median gap/within 50% of median	.670	.661	.658	.660	.663	.654	.640	.648	.652	.649	.643	.637	.637	.631	.636	.636	.639
Below 0.25 median gap/within 50% of median	.857	.849	.839	.837	.861	.848	.842	.834	.831	.832	.832	.827	.834	.842	.839	.842	.844
Bottom-quintile gap/middle 60%	.632	.618	.628	.626	.625	.611	.604	.610	.615	.604	.597	.589	.587	.583	.587	.585	.587
Bottom-decile gap/middle 60%	.748	.733	.734	.737	.737	.722	.712	.719	.725	.712	.704	.695	.693	.684	.693	.691	.693
Weighted Proportional Mean Income Gap																	
Below 0.75 median gap/within 50% of median	.196	.191	.199	.193	.195	.190	.190	.193	.197	.191	.188	.184	.181	.178	.182	.182	.183
Below 0.50 median gap/within 50% of median	.130	.123	.131	.129	.127	.119	.116	.119	.123	.115	.111	.105	.106	.104	.106	.104	.104
Below 0.25 median gap/within 50% of median	.042	.038	.038	.039	.037	.034	.032	.036	.038	.033	.030	.029	.028	.023	.026	.025	.024
Bottom-quintile gap/middle 60%	.158	.155	.157	.156	.156	.153	.151	.152	.154	.151	.149	.147	.147	.146	.147	.146	.147
Bottom-decile gap/middle 60%	.093	.092	.092	.092	.092	.090	.089	.090	.091	.089	.088	.087	.087	.086	.087	.086	.087

Source: Statistics Canada, cat. 13-207, various issues; figures have been calculated using an interpolation program designed by the authors (see Beach and Slotsve 1993 for details).

plus one additional reason. Because of progressive tax rates, when incomes fall, after-tax incomes fall less than proportionally and income losses are buffered by the tax system. The significant rise in income tax rates in the 1980s augments this buffering effect and thus dampens the degree of economic insecurity. All rows in the middle panel of Table 21 show a marked downward trend in the proportional mean income gap. Also, the gap between the incidence figures in Table 20 and those in Table 21 widens substantially as tax rates rise in the 1980s, so the random incidence of substantial losses is reduced.

Similar economic insecurity indexes have also been calculated for individual men and women income recipients. These are provided in Tables 22 and 23, both of which are based on pre-tax incomes. The most dramatic point to note here is that these figures, particularly those on the *incidence* of loss (see the top panel) and even more particularly those on the incidence of *catastrophic* loss (see the top panel's third row), are much higher for individuals than those already seen for families — again confirming the risk-pooling effect of multiple earners within a family. For the composite insecurity indexes in the bottom panels of Tables 22 and 23, one also notes that, at the beginning of the period in the 1970s, economic insecurity figures were generally higher for women than for men. But by the later 1980s they had declined, becoming not much different from the economic insecurity figures for men. Most of this decline appears to have been due to a decreasing random incidence index or decreased income polarization for women. By the mid- to late 1980s, the degree of economic insecurity of men's and women's incomes had generally converged.

The patterns of changes in the indexes for men are rather different from those for women. The indexes for women all peaked in 1976 or shortly thereafter and generally decreased throughout the 1980s; after stabilizing in the 1990–92 recession, they then started to shift up slightly. The incidence and composite indexes for men, on the other hand, generally increased over the 1974–84

Table 22: Alternative Indexes of Economic Insecurity for Female Income Recipients, Canada, Selected Years 1972–92

	1972	1974	1976	1978	1980	1981	1982	1983	1984	1985	1986	1987	1988	1989	1990	1991	1992
Population Shares (percent)																	
Below 0.75 of median/ below 1.50 of median	.612	.598	.639	.618	.590	.586	.572	.562	.556	.555	.545	.558	.549	.548	.537	.539	.550
Below 0.50 of median/ below 1.50 of median	.412	.412	.437	.415	.394	.390	.380	.387	.368	.367	.355	.366	.343	.349	.341	.341	.351
Below 0.25 of median/ Below 1.50 of median	.225	.203	.235	.232	.215	.212	.205	.213	.204	.201	.183	.189	.169	.175	.163	.164	.178
Proportional Mean Income Gap																	
Below 0.75 median gap/ within 50% of median	.604	.607	.607	.611	.606	.605	.601	.614	.607	.608	.596	.599	.578	.589	.583	.580	.587
Below 0.50 median gap/ within 50% of median	.746	.734	.739	.753	.748	.747	.743	.745	.751	.748	.737	.739	.729	.733	.726	.725	.734
Below 0.25 median gap/ within 50% of median	.868	.875	.864	.870	.877	.872	.866	.870	.875	.874	.871	.872	.869	.871	.869	.868	.872
Bottom-quintile gap/ middle 60%	.844	.830	.848	.849	.841	.836	.828	.835	.831	.828	.811	.816	.797	.801	.791	.792	.806
Bottom-decile gap/ middle 60%	.924	.921	.925	.927	.929	.923	.916	.923	.924	.921	.910	.913	.902	.905	.897	.897	.909
Weighted Proportional Mean Income Gap																	
Below 0.75 median gap/ within 50% of median	.370	.363	.388	.378	.358	.355	.344	.345	.338	.337	.325	.334	.317	.323	.313	.313	.323
Below 0.50 median gap/ within 50% of median	.307	.302	.323	.313	.295	.291	.282	.288	.276	.275	.262	.271	.250	.256	.248	.247	.258
Below 0.25 median gap/ within 50% of median	.195	.178	.203	.202	.189	.185	.178	.185	.179	.176	.159	.165	.147	.152	.142	.142	.155
Bottom-quintile gap/ middle 60%	.211	.208	.212	.212	.210	.209	.207	.209	.208	.207	.203	.204	.199	.200	.198	.198	.202
Bottom-decile gap/ middle 60%	.116	.115	.116	.116	.116	.115	.115	.115	.116	.115	.114	.114	.113	.113	.112	.112	.114

Source: Statistics Canada, cat. 13-207, various issues; figures have been calculated using an interpolation program designed by the authors (see Beach and Slotsve 1993 for details).

Table 23: Alternative Indexes of Economic Insecurity for Male Income Recipients, Canada, Selected Years 1972–92

	1972	1974	1976	1978	1980	1981	1982	1983	1984	1985	1986	1987	1988	1989	1990	1991	1992
Population Shares (percent)																	
Below 0.75 of median/ below 1.50 of median	.500	.496	.506	.520	.524	.520	.538	.567	.567	.558	.556	.554	.540	.529	.528	.536	.541
Below 0.50 of median/ below 1.50 of median	.345	.341	.352	.368	.369	.360	.371	.387	.387	.372	.367	.367	.357	.339	.348	.347	.357
Below 0.25 of median/ below 1.50 of median	.178	.165	.169	.175	.178	.164	.171	.183	.183	.170	.167	.172	.163	.145	.161	.153	.163
Proportional Mean Income Gap																	
Below 0.75 median gap/ within 50% of median	.639	.631	.633	.642	.640	.629	.625	.617	.618	.606	.602	.604	.603	.591	.606	.596	.605
Below 0.50 median gap/ within 50% of median	.756	.748	.745	.751	.750	.741	.739	.736	.738	.731	.729	.731	.730	.721	.732	.723	.731
Below 0.25 median gap/ within 50% of median	.869	.869	.869	.873	.879	.877	.880	.879	.883	.876	.874	.872	.869	.869	.872	.870	.880
Bottom-quintile gap/ middle 60%	.810	.799	.801	.810	.813	.800	.807	.815	.817	.805	.799	.802	.794	.776	.792	.783	.796
Bottom-decile gap/ middle 60%	.900	.892	.894	.901	.909	.899	.907	.914	.918	.906	.901	.901	.893	.880	.894	.887	.905
Weighted Proportional Mean Income Gap																	
Below 0.75 median gap/ within 50% of median	.320	.313	.320	.334	.335	.327	.336	.350	.350	.338	.335	.335	.326	.313	.320	.320	.327
Below 0.50 median gap/ within 50% of median	.261	.255	.262	.276	.277	.267	.274	.285	.286	.272	.268	.268	.261	.244	.255	.251	.261
Below 0.25 median gap/ within 50% of median	.155	.143	.147	.153	.157	.144	.151	.161	.162	.149	.146	.150	.142	.126	.140	.133	.143
Bottom-quintile gap/ middle 60%	.203	.200	.200	.203	.203	.200	.202	.204	.204	.201	.200	.201	.199	.194	.198	.196	.199
Bottom-decile gap/ middle 60%	.113	.112	.112	.113	.114	.112	.113	.114	.115	.113	.113	.113	.112	.110	.112	.111	.113

Source: Statistics Canada, cat. 13-207, various issues; figures have been calculated using an interpolation program designed by the authors (see Beach and Slotsve 1993 for details).

period and then declined with the broad expansion over the rest of the 1980s, also bouncing up somewhat in the 1990–92 recession. For men, polarization changes appear to be driving the economic insecurity results; for women, income inequality changes are also important contributing factors.

To review the major results in this section on economic insecurity, the random incidence of economic insecurity for family incomes rose noticeably over the 1974–85 period for moderate to substantial income losses, but there has been a competing long-run downward trend against catastrophic falls in family income. The random incidence of moderate to substantial income losses was about the same for the two major recessions examined, but that of catastrophic losses was much less in the 1990–92 recession. Economic insecurity indexes (particularly those that reflect random incidence of loss) are much higher for individuals than for families, which can pool income risks across earners. There are also quite different economic insecurity patterns for men and women: men experienced a strong rise in incidence of economic insecurity over the 1974–84 period, while women's indexes of insecurity generally decreased through the 1980s. By the late 1980s, men's and women's incomes faced similar degrees of economic insecurity.

Chapter 6

Review and Conclusion

In this study, we have sought to set out the basic evidence on changes in income distribution in Canada over the past 20 years. In particular, we measured the degree to which polarization has occurred in income distribution, as well as the extent to which the middle class declined during the 1980s. We also examined the distributional effect of the increased personal income tax burden, and we estimated the economic insecurity of Canadians. We also considered the extent to which any observed changes in polarization of incomes essentially have been driven by cyclical factors in the labor market, or whether there is an ongoing underlying trend (so that the changes are likely to persist).

We have concentrated on income polarization and on its converse, the income of the so-called middle class. But why should we be concerned about income polarization, as opposed to, say, looking at just the mean or median incomes in a population? There seem to be four concerns here.

First, one aspect of polarization is the incidence of persons with low incomes or with expectations of potentially lowered incomes. If some people are advancing up the distribution, especially on the basis of their own skills and effort, why should there be a concern? But if others are slipping down the distribution into privation and poverty, especially on the basis of changes over which they have no influence — say, technological change or trade adjustment in the labor market — these people can suffer a major loss of standard of living and economic well-being. Greater job anxiety and reduced expectations of economic security may reduce consumer spending and weaken the current economic expansion. The ranks of the working poor may increase, and new entrants to the labor force may face markedly reduced economic opportunities. They and the children brought up in their households may also suffer human costs and face narrowed prospects for fully developing their worthwhile skills in the future, and society can be poorer as a consequence. More concern about economic well-being is thus attributed to polarization at the bottom end of the distribution than at the top.

The second concern has its roots in the sense of fairness and other values that underlie modern liberal democracies ("Slicing the Cake" 1994). A widening gap between rich and poor may weaken equality before the law and reduce participation in the political process, which sets the rules and affects policies that can have winners and losers in society. A more fissured, economically split society may have fewer shared values of fair process.

The third concern stems from a sense of belonging to a large common group, such as some vaguely defined middle class. A more economically polarized society may be a more fractious, less stable society that lacks a consensus perspective and a generally accepted mode of political and social intercourse. The result may be what Robert Reich calls "the revolt of the anxious class" (Manegold 1994, A5). A "community of communities" may find that it has more difficulty functioning smoothly than one that operates on more ready consensus of shared economic values.

A final concern is reflected in a recent strand of economics literature that argues that income inequality may be harmful for economic growth in a democratic economy (Alesina and Rodrik 1994; Persson and Tabellini 1994). Essentially, this argument maintains, the accumulation of the productive capital (human and nonhuman) that drives economic growth may be inhibited by tax and regulatory policies; these policies blunt private returns on such capital in order to reduce concerns regarding distributional inequality and in order to accommodate median-voter preferences for protecting the return on their capital holdings.

A great deal of debate in the distribution area is expressed in terms of income inequality rather than polarization. Why look at polarization specifically? Polarization, or the presence of income recipients at the two ends of the distribution, can be viewed as an extreme version of the more general term "inequality," which describes income differences. But this is the aspect of income inequality that much of the public debate cited at the beginning of this study focuses on. Since little formal analysis of the evidence on income polarization is available, it seems appropriate to address the concept that is the focus of such debate. Taking this approach also serves to sharpen attention toward, and potential policy interest in, economic mobility — particularly downward economic mobility — and economic insecurity, concepts that are not well captured by the more diffuse concept of inequality. Polarization better highlights the dynamics of year-to-year distributional change and one's location in the distribution.

In this study, we have examined a great deal of empirical evidence on income polarization in Canada over the past 20 years. It may be useful to highlight several of the major findings here.

- There has been a marked flattening in the growth of real incomes since the 1970s. For example, the average annual rate of growth in median family incomes was 4.01 percent over the 1965–71 period, 2.65 percent over 1971–80, 0.44 percent over 1980–92, and 0.15 percent over 1986–92. Women's incomes rose steadily over the period, while men's real incomes peaked in 1976 and have not regained that peak since. As a result, the ratio of median incomes of women to men rose from 32 percent to 57 percent over 1965–92.

- The degree of polarization of women's earnings and income is higher than for men's. During the 1980s, the polarization of women's earnings varied similarly to men's but in a far less marked fashion. Beginning in 1976, however, there was a strong downward trend in women's income polarization that lasted until 1990 (Figure 10), reflecting the growing labor market attachment of women and the increased role of transfer income, particularly to women with dependent children at the lower end of the income distribution.

- Men, however, have experienced a quite different pattern of polarization changes. Polarization rates began drifting up in the middle 1970s, jumped up dramatically in the 1981–84 period, drifted partway down during the 1984–89 expansion, and then moved up again between 1989 and 1992 (Figure 7). Clearly, the 1980s and early 1990s were a far more volatile period of polarization change than the 1970s. Polarization in the 1980s was also much more of an issue for men than for women — between 1981 and 1992, earnings polarization rates changed by 1.2 to 2.6 percentage points for women, but increased by 8.5 to 9.0 percentage points for men. Income polarization for men follows a generally similar pattern as that for earnings, but the changes are more damped.

- The sources of polarization change also differ between men and women. The decreasing polarization rates for women from 1976 through 1992 were driven principally by declines in the population shares toward the bottom end of the distribution. Even abstracting from cyclical factors, income polarization rates for women are estimated to have declined by about half a percentage point a year over the 1972–92 period. For men, on the other hand, higher polarization rates in earnings arose from increased proportions of workers at both the upper and the lower ends of the distribution; about one-third to two-fifths of the polarization increases arose from downgrading or slippage in earnings, while more than half stemmed from upgrading of earnings as workers moved into higher regions of the distribution. Also, cyclical factors appear to have essentially driven the polarization changes for men; indeed, when one nets out the effect of cyclical factors, there remains no significant underlying trend in the polarization rate of men's incomes. Thus, while the reduction in polarization of women's incomes appears to be a long-term trend, the increases in polarization rates for men's incomes appear to be more related to slow growth and weak labor markets.

- The converse of polarization is the proportion of persons in the middle range of the distribution, or the so-called middle class. Middle-class shares for men and women converged dramatically between the middle 1970s and the middle 1980s as the proportions with middle-class incomes fell for men and rose for women (Figure 11). Again, cyclical factors appear to have been the driving force behind changes in men's middle-class share, with a 1.0 percentage point fall in the unemployment rate estimated to increase their share by 0.77 of a percentage point. While women's middle-class incomes are still well below those of men's, they grew quite steadily over the 1971–92 period (Figure 12). Men's middle-class incomes, in contrast, declined from their 1976 peak until, by 1992, they were on a par with where they had been two decades earlier, in 1971–72 (Figure 13).

- Family polarization rates are substantially less than those for individual men and women and have more damped year-to-year fluctuations, reflecting the income-pooling role of families. Family polarization rates also changed far less in the 1980s than did the individual rates for men and women, with the most marked change being a moderate increase between 1974 and 1985. Evidently, the opposing patterns of polarization shifts between men and women have tended to net each other out, so that no significant long-run trend remains (Figure 14). The proportion of families in the lower-income group shows both a significant downward trend and a significant cyclical effect similar to, though more damped from, that of individual men. The downward trend probably arises from the increasing role of transfers in family incomes.

- Gains in individual and family incomes vary widely among different demographic or skill groups. During the 1980s, young cohorts of workers experienced real income losses, while peak-age earners, the university educated, and the elderly experienced the largest income gains. Among families, the most marked differences occurred among age groups: between 1980 and 1991, the real income of families with young heads (aged 20–24) fell by 18 percent, while that of families with older heads (aged 65 and over) rose by more than 25 percent.

• Again, the converse of polarization is the middle class, and family income is the conventional basis for identifying the middle class. By the early 1990s, the proportional size of the middle class in Canada was slightly smaller than it had been in the early 1970s. But the most marked declines in the size of the middle class occurred over the 1974–85 period; a further decline set in after 1989 (Figure 15). Again, however, this decline appears to have been driven by cyclical factors. Each percentage point fall in the unemployment rate is estimated to raise the proportion of families in the middle by about one-third of a percentage point. Once such cyclical factors are netted out, no significant downward trend remains. By 1992, the mean incomes of the middle class were barely different from what they had been in the late 1970s (Figure 16).

• The average income tax burden rose substantially over the 1980s, increasing by about 25 percent between 1980 and 1992. Median family after-tax income essentially did not grow at all in the 1980s and was virtually the same in 1992 as it had been in 1976 (Figure 19). The increase in the personal tax burden over the 1980–92 period varied across the income distribution, from a 9 percent increase for the second quintile to a 29 percent increase for the top quintile of families. The effective income tax burden on the middle class increased less in the 1980s than did the average tax rate for families as a whole or that for upper-income families in particular.

- Estimates of what we have called random incidence of economic insecurity for family incomes rose noticeably over the 1974–85 period for moderate to substantial income losses, but there was a competing long-term downward trend against catastrophic falls in family income. There were also quite different economic insecurity patterns for men than for women. Men experienced a strong rise in the incidence of economic insecurity over the 1974–85 period, while economic insecurity indexes for women generally decreased through the 1980s. By the late 1980s, men's and women's incomes faced similar degrees of economic insecurity.

To the question posed in the title of this study — Are We Becoming Two Societies? — the answer suggested by the evidence is "no." The 1980s saw much more marked changes in polarization rates than did the 1970s. But the changes were concentrated primarily in two periods, 1974–85 and 1989–92. They were also heavily affected by standard business cycle fluctuations, particularly by the two severe recessions at opposite ends of the decade. The 1980s were not so much a new era of polarization in Canada as an era of slower economic growth, higher taxes, and two severe recessions that had marked distributional effects.

The shifting of workers into both the upper and the lower ends of the earnings distribution evidenced for men is consistent with both the Deindustrialization/Opening Economy Hypothesis and the Technological Change Hypothesis reviewed in Chapter 1. For women, other factors appear to be playing a more dominant role at the lower end of their earnings distribution; such factors include steadily rising wages for women and the growing attachment of women to the full-time labor market. Both of the above hypotheses essentially operate through the demand side of the labor market. The evident importance of cyclical effects on the polarization of men's earnings also reinforces the importance of demand-side influences on income changes. Yet, as such commentators as Gordon Betcherman and Lars Osberg[1] have pointed out, the recent federal green paper of proposals on social policy reform (Canada 1994) focuses principally on supply-side issues that affect people's incomes. Our results suggest that policy should perhaps address the demand side as well, producing a more balanced package. Chief among demand-side concerns should be efforts directed at long-run tightening of the labor market, given the benefits this approach provides for low-income workers and middle-class families in the economy.

We have found that a significant portion of the increased polarization of men's earnings between 1972 and 1992 arose from a shift of workers down to the lower end of a distribution whose mean and median were by 1992 no higher than they had been in the mid-1970s. These workers are clearly not as well off as were their counterparts in the late 1970s. But who exactly are these workers, and what are their characteristics? The answers to those questions will allow policies to be more precisely targeted at them. To arrive at such answers, we need access to more detailed data on income and earnings by region, by industry and occupation, and by hours and weeks worked. Specifically, we need panel data that follow workers' mobility through time in order to identify the extent to which such a shift of workers in the distribution arises from incumbent workers' losing jobs and income as they slide down the distribution or from new cohorts' entering the distribution at lower incomes than did their predecessors. Unfortunately, available Canadian data cannot answer this question. We thus end this study with a plea for access to more detailed Canadian data in this area so that more precisely focused policies can be developed.

---

1 Commentators at an October 1994 roundtable conference on "Social Policy Reform: The Federal Discussion Paper," held at the School of Policy Studies, Queen's University, Kingston, Ontario.

Appendix

Measuring Inequality and Polarization

Measure of Inequality

A large body of literature exists in economics and statistics on alternative ways to measure income inequality in a distribution of income. Broadly speaking, there are two approaches to measuring income inequality. The first looks at various summary or aggregative measures of inequality, which summarize the degree of inequality in a distribution by a single number. Four leading summary inequality measures are the coefficient of variation, the mean log deviation, Theil's entropy index, and the Gini coefficient. The last three appear in Table 1. If the income distribution consists of N persons or families with income, and their incomes are represented by Yi for the ith person or family, then these four summary measures can be calculated from the following formulas:

$$\text{Coefficient of variation} \ = \ \sqrt{avg\,[\,(Yi - \overline{Y})^2\,]}\ /\ \overline{Y}$$

$$\text{Mean log deviation} \ = \ avg\,[\,(\,\log Yi - \log \overline{Y}\,)^2\,]$$

$$\text{Entropy index} \ = \ avg\,[\,(\tfrac{Yi}{\overline{Y}})\cdot\log(\tfrac{Yi}{\overline{Y}})\,]$$

$$\text{Gini coefficient} \ = \ [\,avg\,|Yi - Yj\,|\,]/2\overline{Y}$$

Here $\overline{Y}$ means the average or mean value of the Yis in the distribution, and $avg\,(\cdot)$ means the average value of the expression within the parentheses — again, averaged over all N persons or families in the distribution. $|\cdot|$ means the absolute value of the differences in incomes. Of these four measures, the Gini coefficient is by far the most frequently used and has the convenient property of lying between the lower bound of zero (that is, no inequality at all, since all N persons in the distribution have identical incomes) and an upper bound of one (the opposite extreme, where one person in the distribution has all the income and the remaining $N - 1$ persons have no income). For all four measures, smaller values indicate a lesser degree of inequality and larger values correspond to a greater degree of inequality.

By its nature, however, any summary measure of inequality averages income differences across the full range of the distribution and thus hides a lot of detail — as to whether, for example, the degree of income inequality is more extreme at one end of the distribution than at the other. To bring out this greater distributional detail, analysts also make use of various disaggregative measures of inequality. Quintile or decile income shares, illustrated in Tables 1 and 4, are examples of such disaggregative measures. To calculate these shares, order the N incomes in the distribution from the lowest-income value to the highest-income value. Then, in the case of quintile shares, divide the ordered income values into fifths: the lowest 20 percent of incomes, the next 20 percent of incomes, and so on, up to the highest 20 percent of income. The income-level cutoff that divides the first from the second quintile group is called the bottom or first quintile income level; the cutoff that separates the second-top from the top quintile group is called the top or fourth quintile income level. The mean income level of each quintile group is the quintile mean for the group. Analogously, the mean of each decile group, if the distribution is divided into ten (ordered) deciles, is the decile mean income level of the group — as illustrated in Table 4. The decile share for each group is the proportion of total income in the distribution that is received by members of this decile group. Higher decile groups have higher income shares, and the sum of

Figure A-1: *Illustrative Lorenz Curve*

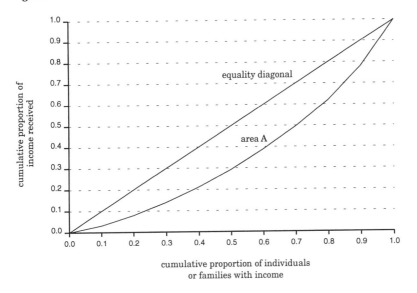

the income shares across all decile groups in the distribution is 100 percent.

If one cumulates the income shares, one gets a Lorenz curve. That is, suppose again that one divides a distribution into ten decile groups. Then, for the lowest decile group, calculate its decile share; for the lowest 20 percent or two decile groups, calculate their income share; for the lowest 30 percent, compute its income share; and so on as one cumulates up the distribution. The Lorenz curve, illustrated in Figure A-1, then graphs the cumulated income shares on the vertical axis corresponding to the cumulated decile proportion (or population shares) on the horizontal axis. If everyone in the distribution received exactly the same income, the Lorenz curve would coincide with the straight diagonal line in Figure A-1 (the *equality diagonal*). At the opposite extreme, if all income resided in only one person's hands, the Lorenz curve would coincide with the bottom and right-hand borders of Figure A-1. The typical Lorenz curve is like the one illustrated, which lies somewhere between these two limiting cases. The closer the Lorenz curve is to the equality diagonal, the less is the degree of inequality in a distribution. Interestingly, when area A in Figure A-1 — the area between the Lorenz curve and the equality diagonal — is divided by the total area beneath the equality diagonal (or one-half), it turns out to be precisely the value of the Gini coefficient defined above. In other words, the Gini coefficient is equal to twice the area between the Lorenz curve for a distribution and the equality diagonal. This simple geometric interpretation of the Gini coefficient is one further reason for the popularity of the Gini coefficient in applied work on inequality.

Income Class Measures and Polarization

Polarization focuses on population shares at the two ends of the distribution. It is thus useful to divide a distribution into only three regions: a lower-income region, a middle-income (or middle-class) region, and an upper-income region. One way to do so is to use cutoffs between the three regions that are based on the median or middle-income level for the distribution. Figure A-2, for example, illustrates cutoffs that are 50 percent of the median and 150 percent of the median. Within each of the three regions of the distribution, one can then calculate both the proportion of individuals or families in that region (the population share) and the proportion of total income in the distribution that is received by members of that region (the income share). If Ng is the number of individuals or families in income group g, the population share of the group is Ng/N. If $\overline{Yg}$ is the mean income of members in income group g, the income share of the group is

$$\frac{(Ng\,\overline{Yg})}{(N\overline{Y})} = \frac{(Ng)}{(N)} \cdot \frac{(\overline{Yg})}{(\overline{Y})},$$

which can be seen to be the product of the population share and a relative income differential; the first term can be thought of as

Figure A-2: *Illustrative Income Distribution*

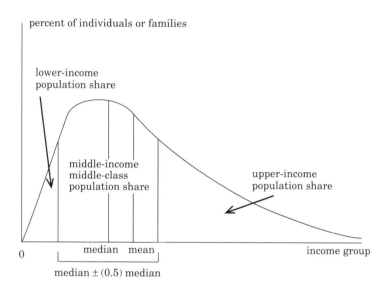

Note: In this figure, "median" denotes "the income such that half of individuals or families in the distribution are poorer and half have higher incomes," while "mean" denotes "the average of all incomes (total income divided by number of individuals or families) in the distribution." If, as is usual, the income distribution has a long right-hand tail, then the mean income exceeds the median income.

capturing an incidence or polarization dimension, while the second term highlights income inequality between groups. Consequently, it can be shown that the year-to-year percentage growth rate in income shares is equal to the sum of the percentage growth rates in population shares and those in the relative income ratio. That is, the percentage change in share of income of group g = the percentage change in population share of group g + the percentage change in mean income of group g relative to the mean income of the whole distribution. Thus, if the income share of some group — say, men with incomes above twice the median — rose by 39 percent (see Table 7, bottom row) between 1972 and 1992 and their population share rose by 54 percent (see Table 7, row 7),

Figure A-3:   *Illustration of a Case of Increased Degree
of Polarization in an Income Distribution*

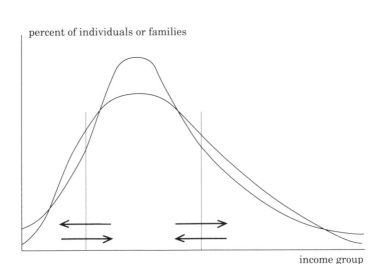

then the group's mean income level fell by 15 percent relative to the mean income of men as a whole over the period.

Since polarization refers to the population shares at the two ends of the distribution, one can illustrate how polarization relates to inequality of income. Figure A-3 illustrates how a distribution can change through shifts of persons away from the middle-lower and the middle-upper ranges into either one of the two ends or the middle range of the distribution. The result is that a summary measure of inequality based on average deviations from the mean will not change (since some medium-sized income deviations are replaced by more larger and smaller income deviations) but the degree of polarization has increased, since there are more persons with extremely high or extremely low incomes. Obviously, however, a shift from the middle-class region to the top and bottom ends of the distribution will increase both polarization and inequality.

Figure A-4:   ***Illustrative Histogram of Population Shares by Income Interval Distribution***

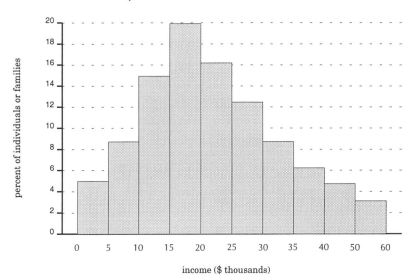

income ($ thousands)

A final matter involves the way that the distribution data used in this study are available in published form. Statistics Canada data typically are provided in the form of a table that indicates the proportion of the population whose incomes lie within various income intervals. For example, Table A-11 shows the type of data that are the basis of the results in this study. The graphical representation of such income group frequency data is a "histogram" diagram, which is illustrated for a typically shaped income distribution in Figure A-4.

For more detailed discussion of measuring and interpreting inequality measures, see Cowell (1977), Osberg (1981), Gunderson (1983), and Jenkins (1991).

Since the estimation procedure we use in this study is based on interpolation of published histogram data, one would expect some form of interpolation errors to exist in the reported inequality and polarization results. However, because the actual microdata in Statistics Canada's Survey of Consumer Finances are not readily available to researchers, it is hard to establish how severe such errors may be. Luckily, however, some basis of comparison between microdata-based and interpolation-based estimates does exist. As part of another study being done at the C.D. Howe Institute, Statistics Canada provided microdata-based estimates of decile mean earnings of full-time, full-year men workers for several years between 1975 and 1992. At the same time, an appendix in Beach and Slotsve (1994) presents interpolation-based estimates of exactly the same decile means. The computer program used in Beach and Slotsve (1994) is the same as that used in this study. A comparison of the two sets of estimates (and the median earnings level) is provided in Table A-12 for the most recent year available (1991). It can be seen that, except for the bottom decile and the top two deciles, the two sets of decile mean estimates differ by less than 2 percent. The decile means at the two ends of the distribution differ by 5 percent to 7 percent. However, since the lowest-decile mean is overestimated and the top-decile mean is underestimated, one would expect that summary measures of inequality would tend to be underestimated by the interpolation program used in this study.

But these results do not throw any light on errors in estimating polarization. *A priori*, though, one may obtain some predictions. In a typical continuous income or earnings distribution (such as that illustrated in Figure A-2), the upward-sloping portion of the curve has a rising slope over lower portions of the distribution, while the downward-sloping portion of the curve has a flattening slope over the top right-hand portion of the distribution. The computer algorithm used in this study, however, is based on *linear* interpolation over these regions. Since the median appears to be estimated quite accurately (see the bottom row of Table A-12), the cutoffs used for the polarization estimates (for example, 0.5 times the median or 1.75 times the median) would also appear to be quite accurately estimated. Thus, the issue of polarization error amounts to establishing error in calculating population shares or the area under the income distribution curve to the left of the lower cutoff level and to the right of the upper cutoff level. Since the income distribution curve's slope typically is rising over this lower region, a linear interpolation procedure will tend to underestimate population shares at the bottom end of the distribution. Conversely, since the income distribution curve's slope typically is flattening out over the upper region, a linear interpolation procedure will tend to overestimate population shares at the top end of the distribution. And since the income distribution curve over the middle region of the distribution both rises and falls within the region, the population share of the middle-class region is not likely to be affected very much by linear interpolation errors. In summary, then, one would expect lower-end population shares to be underestimated and upper-end population shares to be overestimated. The polarization rate or sum of the two population shares combines the two counteracting errors and thus is likely to be subject to a relatively smaller error than its two components. The population share of the middle class, as the converse of the polarization rate, is also likely to be subject to relatively smaller errors than the two extreme population shares.

Table A-1: **Regression Results on Mean and Median Incomes of Individuals, Canada, 1972–92**

	Women		Men	
	Mean Income	**Median Income**	**Mean Income**	**Median Income**
	(figures in parentheses are absolute t-ratios)			
T	0.0202	0.0250	0.0031	0.0004
	(12.3)	(15.0)	(1.96)	(0.22)
UR	− 0.0062	− 0.0150	− 0.0147	− 0.0206
	(1.31)	(3.12)	(3.26)	(3.71)
constant	9.47	9.21	10.38	10.32
	(475.0)	(454.0)	(547.0)	(443.0)
R^2	0.9493	0.9593	0.3928	0.6483
F-stat.	168.4	212.2	5.82	16.59
Mean dependent variable	9.66	9.39	10.32	10.20
NOBS	21	21	21	21

Notes: The dependent variables are the logs of mean and median real incomes of individual men and women income recipients.

The variable T is a linear time trend, and UR is the national unemployment rate (as a percentage) of adult males aged 25 and over.

Table A-2: *Regression Results on Polarization Indexes and Population Shares of Individual Earners, Canada, 1971–92*

	Women			Men		
	Polarization Index	Lower Share	Upper Share	Polarization Index	Lower Share	Upper Share
	(figures in parentheses are absolute t-ratios)					
T	– 0.2742	– 0.2424	– 0.0322	0.1270	– 0.0010	0.0941
	(5.83)	(11.6)	(0.94)	(2.91)	(0.04)	(2.68)
UR	0.8746	0.2192	0.6882	1.3496	0.6603	0.5975
	(5.98)	(3.38)	(6.49)	(9.96)	(8.65)	(5.47)
DPI1	21.14			19.85		
	(53.5)			(54.2)		
DPSL2		13.16			11.31	
		(75.0)			(54.8)	
DPSU2			– 8.01			– 8.54
			(22.8)			(23.6)
DPSU3			– 14.51			– 14.09
			(41.3)			(38.9)
constant	40.12	19.18	28.72	23.56	11.82	21.39
	(52.0)	(56.0)	(49.7)	(32.9)	(29.4)	(35.9)
R^2	0.9918	0.9959	0.9796	0.9926	0.9924	0.9781
F-stat.	967.0	1938.0	444.8	1077.0	1050.0	412.9
Mean dependent variable	53.07	24.05	25.53	44.47	22.01	19.21
NOBS	28	28	42	28	28	42

Notes to Table

The dependent variables in the polarization equation are the polarization indexes 1 and 2 for the years 1971, 1975, 1979, 1981–82, and 1984–92; these are pooled into one equation with the addition of a dummy variable, DPI1. which distinguishes between the two indexes by taking a value of 1 over polarization index 1 observations and 0 over polarization index 2 observations.

The dependent variables in the "Lower Share" equations are the two lower-population shares pooled over the period 1971–92, but excluding the same years as in the above note. Observations for the two shares are distinguished by the dummy variable DPSL2, which takes a value of 1 over the second (that is, 0.50 of the median) set of share observations and 0 otherwise.

The dependent variables in the "Upper Share" equations are the three upper-population shares pooled over the same years in the period 1971–92. Observations for the three shares are distinguished by the dummy variable DPSU2, which takes a value of 1 over the second (that is, 1.75 of the median) set of share observations and 0 otherwise, and DPSU3, which takes a value of 1 over the third (that is, 2.00 of the median) set of share observations and 0 otherwise.

The variable T is a linear time trend, and UR is the national unemployment rate (as a percentage of adult males aged 25 and over).

Observations are pooled in these regressions to obtain a single set of trend and cyclical effects across several alternative measures. Note that, when observations that are not independent are pooled, standard errors are misleadingly low and t-ratios are misleadingly high. Thus, any coefficients with low t-ratios in these regressions are likely to be not at all statistically significant. A similar comment holds for Tables A-3, A-4, A-6, and A-8.

Table A-3: *Regression Results on Polarization Indexes and Population Shares of Income Recipients, Canada, 1972–92*

	Women			Men		
	Polarization Index	Lower Share	Upper Share	Polarization Index	Lower Share	Upper Share
	(figures in parentheses are absolute t-ratios)					
T	− 0.5092	− 0.2371	− 0.2941	− 0.0700	− 0.1540	0.0305
	(11.8)	(8.94)	(13.2)	(1.17)	(7.12)	(0.61)
UR	0.3740	0.1267	0.3343	0.9969	0.2177	0.9332
	(3.00)	(1.67)	(5.24)	(5.76)	(3.52)	(6.49)
DPI1	18.37			21.96		
	(57.3)			(49.3)		
DPSL2		11.84			13.79	
		(59.2)			(84.6)	
DPSU2			− 6.48			− 8.36
			(31.4)			(18.0)
DPSU3			− 12.26			− 13.64
			(59.5)			(29.4)
constant	44.45	15.10	35.56	26.13	12.60	21.42
	(81.2)	(44.2)	(119)	(34.4)	(45.2)	(31.7)
R^2	0.9893	0.9903	0.9857	0.9850	0.9950	0.9479
F-stat.	1175	1220	945.0	832.6	2407	250.3
Mean dependent variable	50.37	19.13	28.10	42.57	19.12	20.36
NOBS	42	40	60	42	40	60

Notes to Table

The dependent variables in the polarization equation are the polarization indexes 1 and 2 for the 21 years 1972–92 that are pooled into one equation with the addition of a dummy variable, DPI1, which distinguishes between the two indexes by taking a value of 1 over polarization index 1 observations and 0 over polarization index 2 observations.

The dependent variables in the "Lower Share" equations are the two lower-population shares pooled over the period 1972–92, but excluding the year 1975 because of a paucity of income histogram intervals published for that year. Observations for the two shares are distinguished by the dummy variable DPSL2, which takes a value of 1 over the second (that is, 0.50 of the median) set of share observations and 0 otherwise.

The dependent variables in the "Upper Share" equations are the three upper-population shares pooled over the periods 1972–74 and 1976–92. Observations for the three shares are distinguished by the dummy variable DPSU2, which takes a value of 1 over the second (that is, 1.75 of the median) set of share observations and 0 otherwise, and DPSU3, which takes a value of 1 over the third (that is, 2.00 of the median) set of share observations and 0 otherwise.

The variable T is a linear time trend, and UR is the national unemployment rate (as a percentage) of adult males aged 25 and over.

Table A-4: *Regression Results on Population Shares of Middle-Class Individual Income Recipients, Canada, 1972–92*

	Women	Men
	(figures in parentheses are absolute t-ratios)	
T	0.3665	0.0188
	(10.7)	(0.53)
UR	−0.0893	−0.7743
	(0.90)	(7.48)
DMC2	8.49	9.32
	(23.5)	(24.7)
DMC3	28.35	32.16
	(78.6)	(85.4)
DMC4	46.72	54.13
	(129)	(144)
constant	8.62	18.91
	(18.3)	(38.4)
R^2	0.9962	0.9969
F-stat.	4086	5002
Mean dependent variable	32.98	38.19
NOBS	84	84

Note: The dependent variables are the middle-class population shares for the 21 years 1972–92; these are pooled over the first four measures into one equation, with the addition of dummy variables to distinguish among the alternative middle-class share measures. DMC2 takes a value of 1 for observations in the range ± 0.25 of the median and 0 otherwise; DMC3 takes a value of 1 for observations in the range ± 0.50 of the median and 0 otherwise; and DMC4 takes a value of 1 for observations in the range ± 0.75 of the median and 0 otherwise. The default share range is ± 0.15 of the median (that is, the first measure of middle-class share).

The variable T is a linear time trend, and UR is the national unemployment rate (as a percentage) of adult males aged 25 and over.

Table A-5:   *Mean Real Incomes of Middle-Class Income Recipients, Canada, 1972–92*

	Women			Men		
	Between 0.75 and 1.25 of Median	Between 0.50 and 1.50 of Median	Middle 60%	Between 0.75 and 1.25 of Median	Between 0.50 and 1.50 of Median	Middle 60%
			(constant 1991 $)			
1972	8,808	8,360	10,020	26,689	26,579	26,083
1974	9,891	9,569	11,288	28,120	27,848	27,545
1976	10,230	9,614	11,602	29,426	29,217	29,190
1978	11,178	10,713	12,624	28,561	28,592	28,230
1980	11,178	10,754	12,892	28,859	28,677	28,487
1982	11,652	11,218	13,340	26,428	26,053	26,796
1984	11,671	11,265	13,299	24,996	24,325	25,845
1986	12,636	12,111	14,118	25,558	24,805	26,632
1988	13,032	12,550	14,632	26,241	25,624	27,226
1990	14,068	13,636	15,583	26,621	26,024	27,018
1991	13,865	13,324	15,356	25,243	24,497	25,866
1992	13,857	13,374	15,595	25,059	24,448	25,971

Source: Statistics Canada, cat. 13-207, various issues; figures have been calculated using an interpolation program designed by the authors (see Beach and Slotsve 1993 for details).

Table A-6: *Regression Results on Polarization Rate and Population Shares for Families, Canada, 1972–92*

	Polarization Share	Lower Share	Upper Share	Mid-Class Share
	(figures in parentheses are absolute t-ratios)			
T	–0.1150	–0.0932	0.0187	0.0358
	(1.40)	(4.79)	(0.24)	(0.75)
UR	0.3666	0.1614	0.0813	–0.3512
	(1.54)	(2.90)	(0.36)	(2.53)
DPI1	21.13			
	(34.6)			
DPSL2		13.62		
		(93.0)		
DPSU2			–7.52	
			(10.2)	
DPSU3			–11.24	
			(15.3)	
DMC2				12.54
				(24.9)
DMC3				39.31
				(77.9)
DMC4				60.44
				(120.0)
constant	18.44	4.43	21.58	21.89
	(17.7)	(17.7)	(20.2)	(33.2)
R^2	0.9693	0.9959	0.8159	0.9955
F-stat.	399.9	2890.	60.9	3466.
Mean dependent variable	30.03	11.21	16.05	48.16
NOBS	42	40	60	84

Notes to Table

The dependent variables are the logs of mean and median real incomes of individual men and women income recipients.

The variable T is a linear time trend, and UR is the national unemployment rate (as a percentage) of adult males aged 25 and over.

The dependent variables in the polarization equation are the polarization indexes 1 and 2 for the years 1971, 1975, 1979, 1981–82, and 1984–92; these are pooled into one equation with the addition of a dummy variable, DPI1, which distinguishes between the two indexes by taking a value of 1 over polarization index 1 observations and 0 over polarization index 2 observations.

The dependent variables in the "Lower Share" equations are the two lower-population shares pooled over the period 1971–92, but excluding the same years as in the above note. Observations for the two shares are distinguished by the dummy variable DPSL2, which takes a value of 1 over the second (that is, 0.50 of the median) set of share observations and 0 otherwise.

The dependent variables in the "Upper Share" equations are the three upper-population shares pooled over the same years in the period 1971–92. Observations for the three shares are distinguished by the dummy variable DPSU2, which takes a value of 1 over the second (that is, 1.75 of the median) set of share observations and 0 otherwise, and DPSU3, which takes a value of 1 over the third (that is, 2.00 of the median) set of share observations and 0 otherwise.

The variable T is a linear time trend, and UR is the national unemployment rate (as a percentage of adult males aged 25 and over).

Observations are pooled in these regressions to obtain a single set of trend and cyclical effects across several alternative measures. Note that, when observations that are not independent are pooled, standard errors are misleadingly low and t-ratios are misleadingly high. Thus, any coefficients with low t-ratios in these regressions are likely ot be not at all statistically significant. A similar comment holds for Tables A-3, A-4, A-6, and A-8.

Table A-7: *Mean Incomes of Middle-Class Families, Canada, 1972–92*

	Between 0.75 and 1.25 of Median	Between 0.50 and 1.50 of Median	Middle 60% of Families
	(constant 1991 $)		
1972	39,146	38,634	39,149
1973	40,229	39,688	40,980
1974	42,775	42,073	43,025
1975	45,100	42,753	46,845
1976	44,845	44,330	45,642
1977	45,359	44,812	46,194
1978	45,992	45,180	46,740
1979	45,888	43,851	47,648
1980	47,274	46,672	47,556
1981	46,465	45,715	47,121
1982	44,536	43,923	45,577
1983	43,629	42,787	44,791
1984	43,821	42,984	44,298
1985	44,513	43,494	45,407
1986	46,145	45,335	47,068
1987	46,603	45,651	47,674
1988	47,644	46,564	48,766
1989	48,802	47,886	50,068
1990	48,356	47,249	49,398
1991	46,517	45,383	47,733
1992	46,812	45,539	47,680

Source: Statistics Canada, cat. 13-207, various issues; figures have been calculated using an interpolation program designed by the authors (see Beach and Slotsve 1993 for details).

Table A-8:   *Regression Results on Mean and Median Family Incomes and Mean Middle-Class Income, Canada, 1972–92*

	Mean Family Income	Median Family Income	Mean Middle-Class Income
	(figures in parentheses are absolute t-ratios)		
T	0.0129	0.0117	0.0111
	(7.61)	(6.26)	(10.1)
UR	− 0.0157	− 0.0174	− 0.0175
	(3.19)	(3.22)	(5.49)
DMC2			− 0.0195
			(1.94)
DMC3			− 0.0406
			(4.05)
constant	10.78	10.70	10.73
	(522.0)	(470.0)	(736.0)
R^2	0.8143	0.7233	0.6998
F-stat.	39.46	23.52	33.80
Mean dependent variable	10.83	10.72	10.72
NOBS	21	21	63

Note: The dependent variables are the logs of mean and median real family incomes and the log of mean middle-class real incomes. DMC2 takes a value of 1 for observations in the range ± 0.25 of the median and 0 otherwise; DMC3 takes a value of 1 for observations in the range ± 0.50 of the median and 0 otherwise.

      The variable T is a linear time trend, and UR is the national unemployment rate (as a percentage) of adult males aged 25 and over.

Table A-9:   *After-Tax Income and Tax Burden of*
             Individual Income Recipients, Canada, 1971–92

	Men		Women	
	Mean Income	**Tax Burden**	**Mean Income**	**Tax Burden**
	(constant 1991 $)	*(%)*	*(constant 1991 $)*	*(%)*
1971	23,250	16.1	10,262	12.0
1972	24,122	16.4	10,776	12.1
1973	24,620	16.5	11,242	11.0
1974	25,752	16.5	12,003	10.8
1975	25,960	16.3	12,334	9.8
1976	27,360	17.2	12,559	10.6
1977	26,226	16.0	13,400	10.5
1978	26,324	15.9	13,699	10.1
1979	26,088	16.7	13,524	11.0
1980	26,108	17.0	13,743	11.2
1981	25,688	17.0	14,086	11.5
1982	24,892	17.2	13,991	11.9
1983	24,265	17.6	13,728	12.2
1984	23,929	17.5	14,091	12.2
1985	24,458	18.0	14,198	12.7
1986	24,400	19.0	14,397	13.8
1987	23,994	20.3	14,465	14.7
1988	24,485	20.2	14,770	14.6
1989	24,706	21.0	15,302	15.3
1990	24,089	21.6	15,347	15.8
1991	23,403	21.5	15,159	16.0
1992	23,451	20.9	15,586	15.8

Source: After-tax incomes are from Statistics Canada, cat. 13-210, various issues; before-tax incomes are from Statistics Canada, cat. 13-207, various issues. Current incomes have been converted to constant 1991 dollars by the authors (based on the consumer price index).

Table A-10: *Decile Mean After-Tax Income and Decile Shares of Families, Canada, 1972–92*

Decile	1972	1974	1976	1980	1982	1984	1986	1988	1991	1992
	(constant 1991 $; figures in parentheses are decile shares in percentages)									
Bottom	8,535	9,959	10,446	10,714	11,301	10,481	11,733	12,406	12,135	12,137
	(2.4)	(2.5)	(2.5)	(2.5)	(2.7)	(2.6)	(2.7)	(2.8)	(2.8)	(2.8)
2nd	16,363	18,508	18,732	19,815	19,752	18,859	20,178	20,987	20,396	20,516
	(4.5)	(4.7)	(4.4)	(4.6)	(4.7)	(4.6)	(4.7)	(4.8)	(4.8)	(4.8)
3rd	22,370	24,826	25,332	26,691	25,630	24,480	25,927	26,839	25,898	25,984
	(6.2)	(6.2)	(6.0)	(6.1)	(6.1)	(6.0)	(6.0)	(6.1)	(6.1)	(6.1)
4th	27,244	30,084	31,288	32,573	31,139	30,125	31,353	32,212	30,995	31,277
	(7.6)	(7.6)	(7.4)	(7.5)	(7.4)	(7.3)	(7.3)	(7.4)	(7.3)	(7.3)
5th	31,603	34,769	36,412	37,893	36,033	35,296	36,530	37,352	36,012	36,380
	(8.8)	(8.7)	(8.6)	(8.7)	(8.6)	(8.6)	(8.5)	(8.5)	(8.5)	(8.5)
6th	35,654	39,390	41,431	42,918	41,121	40,361	41,752	42,648	41,236	41,678
	(9.9)	(9.9)	(9.8)	(9.9)	(9.8)	(9.8)	(9.7)	(9.8)	(9.7)	(9.8)
7th	40,201	44,154	47,014	48,729	46,711	45,863	47,544	48,351	47,132	47.437
	(11.1)	(11.1)	(11.1)	(11.2)	(11.1)	(11.2)	(11.1)	(11.1)	(11.1)	(11.1)
8th	45,797	50,409	53,761	55,606	54,524	52,577	54,546	55,290	54,000	54,260
	(12.7)	(12.7)	(12.7)	(12.8)	(13.0)	(12.8)	(12.7)	(12.6)	(12.7)	(12.7)
9th	54,449	59,726	64,072	66,544	68,873	63,713	64,149	66,052	67,863	67,877
	(15.1)	(15.0)	(15.1)	(15.3)	(16.4)	(15.5)	(14.9)	(15.1)	(15.9)	(15.9)
							–			
Top	78,625	85,942	95,703	93,176	84,980	89,093	95,949	95,171	90,451	89,613
	(21.8)	(21.6)	(22.6)	(21.4)	(20.2)	(21.7)	(22.3)	(21.8)	(21.2)	(21.0)

Source: Statistics Canada, cat. 13-210, various issues; figures have been calculated using an interpolation program designed by the authors (see Beach and Slotsve 1993 for details).

Table A-11: *Percentage Distribution of Families*
by Income Group, Canada, 1992

Income Group	Percent in Group
Under $10,000	2.4
10,000–14,999	3.8
15,000–19,999	5.9
20,000–24,999	7.5
25,000–29,999	6.7
30,000–34,999	6.6
35,000–39,999	7.1
40,000–44,999	6.3
45,000–49,999	6.6
.	.
.	.
.	.
90,000–99,999	3.8
100,000 and over	7.9
Total	*100.0*

Note: Average family income: $53,676
        Median family income: $47,719

Source: Statistics Canada, cat. 13-207, 1993, 53.

Table A-12: *Decile Mean Earnings of Full-Time, Full-Year Male Workers, Canada, 1991*

Decile	Estimates Based on Statistics Canada Microdata (1)	Estimates Based on Authors' Interpolation Program (2)	Percentage Difference 100 × [(2) – (1)] / (1)
	(1991 $)	(1991 $)	(%)
Bottom	7,884	8,399	+ 6.5
2nd	17,429	17,641	+ 1.2
3rd	23,476	23,743	+ 1.1
4th	28,335	28,635	+ 1.1
5th	32,602	33,009	+ 1.2
6th	37,254	37,548	+ 0.8
7th	42,146	42,637	+ 1.2
8th	48,447	48,986	+ 1.1
9th	56,996	59,019	+ 3.5
Top	91,067	86,053	– 5.5
Median	35,122	35,144	+ 0.06

Sources: Estimates in (1) from special computer runs by Statistics Canada for the C.D. Howe Institute; estimates in (2) from Beach and Slotsve 1994, 339.

References

Alesina, A., and D. Rodrik. 1994. "Distributive Politics and Economic Growth." *Quarterly Journal of Economics* 109 (May): 465–490.

Baldwin, J., and P.K. Gorecki. 1993. "Dimensions of Labor Market Change in Canada: Intersectoral Shifts, Jobs, and Worker Turnover." *Journal of Income Distribution* 3 (fall): 148–180.

Beach, C.M., and G.A. Slotsve. 1993. "Polarization of Earnings in the Canadian Labour Market: A Non-Microdata Approach." Discussion Paper 17. Kingston, Ont.: Queen's University, John Deutsch Institute for the Study of Economic Policy.

———. 1994. "Polarization of Earnings in the Canadian Labor Market." In T.J. Courchene, ed., *Stabilization, Growth and Distribution: Linkages in the Knowledge Era*. Bell Canada Papers on Economic and Public Policy 2. Kingston, Ont.: Queen's University, John Deutsch Institute for the Study of Economic Policy.

Beatty, J. 1994. "Who Speaks for the Middle Class?" *The Atlantic Monthly* (May), pp. 65–78.

Berman, E., J. Bound, and Z. Griliches. 1994. "Changes in the Demand for Skilled Labor within US Manufacturing: Evidence from the Annual Survey of Manufactures." *Quarterly Journal of Economics* 109 (May): 367–398.

Betcherman, G., and R. Morissette. 1993. "Recent Youth Labor Market Experiences in Canada." Paper presented at the Canadian Employment Research Forum workshop on Youth Labor Adjustment, June, Vancouver.

Betts, J., and T.H. McCurdy. 1993. "Sources of Employment Growth by Occupation and Industry in Canada." *Relations Industrielles* 48 (2): 285–304.

Blackburn, M.L., and D.E. Bloom. 1993. "The Distribution of Family Income: Measuring and Explaining Changes in the 1980s for Canada and the United States." In D. Card and R.B. Freeman, eds., *Small Differences That Matter: Labor Markets and Income Maintenance in Canada and the United States*. Chicago: University of Chicago Press for the National Bureau of Economic Research.

————. 1994. "Changes in the Structure of Family Income Inequality in the United States and Other Industrial Nations during the 1980s." Discussion Paper 693. New York: Columbia University, Department of Economics.

Blank, R.M., and M.J. Hanratty. 1993. "Responding to Need: A Comparison of Social Safety Nets in Canada and the United States." In D. Card and R.B. Freeman, eds., *Small Differences That Matter: Labor Markets and Income Maintenance in Canada and the United States*. Chicago: University of Chicago Press for the National Bureau of Economic Research.

Bluestone, B., and B. Harrison. 1988. "The Growth of Low-Wage Employment: 1963–86." *American Economic Review* 78 (May): 124–128.

Bound, J., and G. Johnson. 1992. "Changes in the Structure of Wages in the 1980s: An Evaluation of Alternative Explanations." *American Economic Review* 82 (June): 371–392.

Burbidge, J.B., L. Magee, and A.L. Robb. 1994. "Canadian Wage Inequality over the Last Two Decades." Working Paper 93-07. Hamilton, Ont.: McMaster University, Department of Economics.

Burtless, G., ed. 1990. *A Future of Lousy Jobs: The Changing Structure of US Wages*. Washington, DC: Brookings Institution.

Canada. 1994. Department of Human Resources Development. *Improving Social Security in Canada: A Discussion Paper*. Ottawa: Supply and Services Canada.

Canadian Council on Social Development. 1993. *Family Security in Insecure Times*, vol. 1. Ottawa: CCSD.

Card, D., and R.B. Freeman, eds. 1993. *Small Differences That Matter: Labor Markets and Income Maintenance in Canada and the United States*. Chicago: University of Chicago Press for the National Bureau of Economic Research..

Contenta, S. 1993. "'Taxed to death' middle class takes it out on politicians." *Toronto Star*, September 4, p. A1.

Cook, P. 1994. "Taxation isn't always what it seems." *Globe and Mail* (Toronto), October 31, p. B1.

Cowell, F.A. 1977. *Measuring Inequality*. Oxford: Philip Allan.

Danziger, S., and P. Gottschalk, eds. 1993. *Uneven Tides: Rising Inequality in America*. New York: Russell Sage Foundation.

Dooley, M.D. 1986. "The Overeducated Canadian? Changes in the Relationship among Earnings, Education and Age for Canadian Men, 1971–81." *Canadian Journal of Economics* 19 (1): 142–159.

———. 1987. "Within-Cohort Earnings Inequality among Canadian Men, 1971–82." *Relations Industrielles* 42 (3): 594–609.

———. 1994. "Women, Children and Poverty in Canada." *Canadian Public Policy* 20(4): 430–443.

Duncan, G.J., T.M. Smeeding, and W. Rodgers. 1992a. "The Incredible Shrinking Middle Class." *American Demographics* 14(5): 34–38.

———, T.M. Smeeding, and W. Rodgers. 1992b. *W(h)ither the Middle Class? A Dynamic View.* Policy Studies Paper 1. Syracuse, NY: Syracuse University, Maxwell School of Citizenship and Public Affairs, Metropolitan Studies Program.

Economic Council of Canada. 1990a. *Good Jobs, Bad Jobs: Employment in the Service Economy.* Ottawa: Supply and Services Canada.

———. 1990b. "Skill Composition of Employment." *Au Courant*, February, p. 5.

Esteban, J.M., and D. Ray. 1994. "On the Measurement of Polarization." *Econometrica* 62 (July): 819–852.

Farney, D. 1994. "Why middle-class America is fed up," *Globe and Mail* (Toronto), December 27, p. A15.

Foster, J.E., and M.C. Wolfson. 1993. "Measuring the Middle." Nashville, Tenn., Vanderbilt University, Department of Economics. Mimeographed.

Freeman, A. 1990. "Middle class slowly splits into rich and poor." *Globe and Mail* (Toronto), December 28, p. A1.

Freeman, R.B., and K. Needels. 1993. "Skill Differentials in Canada in an Era of Rising Labor Market Inequality." In D. Card and R.B. Freeman, eds., *Small Differences That Matter: Labor Markets and Income Maintenance in Canada and the United States*, National Bureau of Economic Research. Chicago: University of Chicago Press.

Greenspon, E. 1993. "The incredible, shrinking middle class." *Globe and Mail* (Toronto), July 31, p. D1.

Gunderson, M. 1983. *Economics of Poverty and Income Distribution.* Toronto: Butterworth.

Henderson, D.W., and J.C.R. Rowley. 1977. "The Distribution and Evolution of Canadian Family Incomes, 1965–1973." Discussion Paper 91. Ottawa: Economic Council of Canada.

———, and J.C.R. Rowley. 1978. "Structural Changes and the Distribution of Canadian Family Incomes, 1965–1975." Discussion Paper 118. Ottawa: Economic Council of Canada.

Horner, K., and N. MacLeod. 1980. "Analyzing Postwar Changes in Canadian Income Distribution." In Economic Council of Canada, *Reflections on Canadian Incomes: A Collection of Papers Presented to the Conference on Canadian Incomes, Winnipeg, Manitoba, May 10–12, 1979.* Ottawa: Supply and Services Canada.

"Inequality: For Richer, for Poorer." 1994. *The Economist,* November 5, pp. 19–21.

Jenkins, G. 1991. "The Measurement of Income Inequality." In L. Osberg, ed., *Economic Inequality and Poverty: International Perspectives.* Armonk, NY: M.E. Sharpe.

Karoly, L.A. 1993. "The Trend in Inequality among Families, Individuals, and Workers in the United States: A Twenty-Five-Year Perspective." In S. Danziger and P. Gottschalk, eds., *Uneven Tides: Rising Inequality in America.* New York: Russell Sage Foundation.

Kosters, M.H., and M.N. Ross. 1988. "A Shrinking Middle Class?" *Public Interest* 90 (winter): 3–27.

Leckie, N. 1988. "The Declining Middle and Technological Change: Trends in the Distribution of Employment Income in Canada, 1971–84." Discussion Paper 342. Ottawa: Economic Council of Canada.

Levy, F., and R.C. Michel. 1991. *The Economic Future of American Families: Income and Wealth Trends.* Washington, DC: Urban Institute.

———, and R.J. Murnane. 1992. "US Earnings Levels and Earnings Inequality: A Review of Recent Trends and Proposed Explanations." *Journal of Economic Literature* 30 (September): 1333–1381.

Love, R., and S. Poulin. 1991. "Family Income Inequality in the 1980s." *Canadian Economic Observer* (September): Sect. 4.

McInnes, C. 1990. "Faith in economy hard to come by." *Globe and Mail* (Toronto), December 31, p. A1.

McWatters, C.J., and C.M. Beach. 1990. "Factors behind the Changes in Canada's Family Income Distribution and the Share of the Middle Class." *Relations Industrielles* 45 (1): 118–133.

Manegold, C.S. 1994. "Reich urges executives to aid labor." *New York Times,* September 25, p. A5.

Morissette, R., J. Myles, and G. Picot. 1994a. "Earnings Inequality and the Distribution of Working Time in Canada." *Canadian Business Economics* 2 (spring): 3–16.

———, J. Myles, and G. Picot. 1994b. "Earnings Polarization in Canada 1969–1991." Paper presented at the Conference on Labour Market Polarization and Social Policy, Kingston, Ont., Queen's University, School of Policy Studies. January.

Myles, J. 1987. "The Expanding Middle: Some Canadian Evidence on the Deskilling Debate." Research Paper 9. Ottawa: Statistics Canada, Analytical Studies Branch.

———, G. Picot, and T. Wannell. 1988a. "The Changing Wage Distribution of Jobs, 1981–1986." *Canadian Economic Observer* (November): Sect. 4.

———, G. Picot, and T. Wannell. 1988b. "Wages and Jobs in the 1980s: Changing Youth Wages and the Declining Middle." Research Paper 17. Ottawa: Statistics Canada, Analytical Studies Branch.

National Council of Welfare. 1994. *Poverty Profile 1992*. Cat. H67-1/4-1992E. Ottawa: Supply and Services Canada.

Osberg, L. 1981. *Economic Inequality in Canada*. Toronto: Butterworth.

Persson, T., and G. Tabellini. 1994. "Is Inequality Harmful for Growth?" *American Economic Review* 84 (June): 600–621.

Phillips, K.P. 1993. *Boiling Point*. New York: Random House.

Phipps, S.A. 1994. "Poverty and Labour Market Change: Canada in Comparative Perspective." Paper presented at the Conference on Labour Market Polarization and Social Policy, Kingston, Ont., Queen's University, School of Policy Studies. January.

Quarterly Journal of Economics. 1992. Issue on wage inequality. February.

Rashid, A. 1989. *Family Income*. 1986 Census of Canada. Ottawa: Statistics Canada. Cat. 98-128. July.

Richardson, D.H. 1994. "Changes in the Distribution of Wages in Canada, 1981–1992." Discussion Paper 94-22. Vancouver: University of British Columbia, Department of Economics.

Ross, D.P., E.R. Shillington, and C. Lochhead. 1994. *The Canadian Fact Book on Poverty — 1994*. Ottawa: Canadian Council on Social Development.

Sharpe, A. 1993. "Living Standards in Canada and the United States: A Comparative Analysis." Paper presented at the Canadian Economics Association meetings, Ottawa, Carleton University. June.

"Slicing the Cake." 1994. *The Economist* , November 5, pp. 13–14.

Statistics Canada. Cat. 13-207. *Income Distributions by Size in Canada*. Ottawa. Annual.

———. Cat. 13-210. *Income after Tax, Distributions by Size in Canada*. Ottawa. Annual.

———. Cat. 13-217. *Earnings of Men and Women*. Ottawa. Annual.

Uchitelle, L. 1994. "Insecurity forever: The rise of the losing class." *New York Times*, November 20, p. 4.1.

United States. 1991. 102nd Congress. House of Representatives. Committee on Ways and Means. Subcommittee on Human Resources. "Background Material on Family Income and Benefit Changes." Washington, DC: US Government Printing Office.

Vaillancourt, F. 1994. "Income Distribution, Income Security, and Fiscal Federalism." In K. Banting and D. Brown, eds., *Conference on the Future of Fiscal Federalism*. Kingston, Ont.: Queen's University, School of Policy Studies.

Wells, Jennifer. 1993. "Downwardly mobile." *Globe and Mail Report on Business Magazine*. (May), p. 29.

Wolfson, M.C. 1986. "Stasis amid Change: Income Inequality in Canada 1965–1983." *Review of Income and Wealth* 32 (December): 337–368.

———. 1989. "Inequality and Polarization: Is There a Disappearing Middle Class in Canada?" In *Proceedings of the Statistics Canada Symposium on Analysis of Data in Time*. Ottawa: Statistics Canada.

Wolfson, M.C., and B.B. Murphy. 1993. "Uneven Tides, Eddies and Swirls: Evolving Inequality and Polarization in Canada." Paper presented at the Canadian Economics Association meetings, Ottawa, Carleton University. June.

A Comment

Chris Sarlo

Before undertaking a critical evaluation of the study by Charles Beach and George Slotsve, it is useful to examine generally the complex nature of observed income inequality. Both the distribution of income and the degree of inequality of income are issues of great interest to social scientists. Which groups end up with what share of overall income and how the income distribution shifts over time give us some insight into the changing structure of Canada's economic system. As well, the pattern of inequality may provide useful information about the effectiveness of our income redistribution mechanisms. In Canadian society, redistribution of income proceeds voluntarily and informally within families, charitable groups, and communities, and formally via the state.

The degree of income inequality in society has strong political implications. For example, there is a constituency for the view that income inequality is, by definition, bad. Great differences in the incomes of individuals and families are proof of an unfair system. According to this view, evidence of increasing income inequality is political ammunition in the fight for fundamental changes in the way income and wealth get distributed. An alternative view regards as immoral only those incomes that are obtained by force or by fraud. High earnings that are due to creativity and hard work, therefore, are not just acceptable according to this view, but should be encouraged because they result in great economic benefit to society.

In the quest for greater understanding of the nature of income inequality in Canada — that is, the degree of inequality, the trends in inequality, and, more important, the interpretation of these data — one should examine, at least briefly, what it is that produces differences in incomes. It turns out that there is such a wide variety of influences, with some offsetting others, that it is quite impossible to predict changes in key measures of income inequality.

Explaining Income Inequality

Age demographics explain much of the income inequality in Canada's economy. As a worker ages, earnings from employment, the dominant source of income for most households, typically rise. With age, most workers gain experience, take on more responsibility, and are generally more productive. As their value to the employer increases, so too does (real) pay. Thus, even in a society where every worker has exactly the same *lifetime income,* there will be quite substantial income inequality at any point in time because of wage progress with age.

Skills differentials are another obvious contributor to income inequality. People have different natural capabilities and different levels of education. Those with greater ability and higher education are more likely to acquire higher-paying jobs. It is important to note that the best-paid jobs usually involve not only greater skill, but also greater responsibility and longer working hours — in both the investment phase and the career phase.

While age and skills considerations are the dominant root causes of income inequality in Canada, other factors have an influence as well. For example, cyclical and structural changes in the economy typically will result in a change in the degree of income inequality. The unemployment rate is likely to have a strong but uncertain effect on income inequality, depending on the distribution of layoffs. If the rise in unemployment is predominantly in middle- and lower-income occupations, the incomes of some families in the middle- and lower-middle-income ranges will be sharply reduced, pushing them into lower income deciles. Consequently, there is an increase in measured income inequality. Structural changes such as the loss of middle-class industrial jobs or the substitution of part-time jobs for full-time jobs also tend to increase measured inequality.

Certain demographic changes have predictable effects on income inequality. For example, the rise in the proportion of elderly citizens in the population is likely to increase the degree of inequality, since most retirees experience a sharp reduction in income. As well, the increase in the rate of marital breakdown, in the number and proportion of single-parent families, and in the number and proportion of (independently living) postsecondary students all tend to increase measured income inequality.

On the other hand, some demographic changes have an ambiguous impact on inequality. Increased female participation in the workforce, for example, and the corresponding increase in the number and proportion of two-income families could reduce inequality, although this is dependent on an egalitarian approach to marriage, in which the choice of partner is made completely independent of income level. As Beach and Slotsve point out, an increasing propensity among high- and low-income earners to match with others from the same income group tends to increase family income inequality.

Tracking measures of income inequality shows how this complex mix of influences nets out. The point here is that a variety of factors affects the degree of measured income inequality. It is not at all clear, therefore, that rising inequality, should it be detected, is a sign of increasing unfairness in society. In part, this is because the sociodemographic and economic factors described above can change measured inequality without there being any change in anyone's lifetime income and, in part, because, as already mentioned, there are quite different points of view on what is considered fair or unfair about income inequality.

Table 1 presents the trends in some of the demographic categories that are likely to influence measured income inequality.

Beach and Slotsve present an impressive array of statistical information bearing on the question: What happened to individ-

Table 1:   *Demographic Trends Affecting Inequality, Canada, 1971–91*

Category	1971	1981	1991
Total population (thousands)	21,568	24,343	27,296
Population over age 65 (percent)	8.1	8.0	11.6
Lone-parent families (percent)	9.4	16.6	20.0
Average family size	3.7	3.3	3.1
Female participation rate (percent)	39.4	51.7	58.2
College and university full-time enrollment (percent of total population)	2.2	2.6	3.1

Source: Statistics Canada, *Canada Yearbook*, various issues.

ual and family incomes in Canada over the two decades ending in 1992? Using a multiplicity of measures, they focus particular attention on the issues of income polarization and middle-class shares. Their conclusion — that there is no evidence of any statistically significant trend in either case — is important, and contradicts some popular views about patterns of inequality in Canadian society. It therefore bears repeating: there is *no support* for the claim that the middle class is declining, and there is *nothing to support* the view that family incomes are more unequal or more polarized now than they were 20 years ago.

Beach and Slotsve endeavor to set out the basic evidence for changes in the distribution of Canadian incomes for the 1972–92 period. That they have done! This high-quality study will be a valuable resource, not only for students of inequality, but also — and perhaps most important — for journalists and commentators.

Methodology

Each year, Statistics Canada conducts a Survey of Consumer Finances (SCF), an income survey of some 40,000 Canadian households. Participants are selected randomly so that the data will reflect the entire Canadian population. Beach and Slotsve maintain that the microdata file is not easily accessible to researchers, so they employ grouped data from the published SCF results. They input this grouped data into a computer program that uses an interpolation procedure[1] to compute measures of polarization, decile shares, and middle-class shares.

While the microdata file is considered ideal for many purposes, careful use of grouped data to generate deciles and measures of polarization need not be a disadvantage. Table 2 presents the family decile shares for 1990 (expressed in 1991 dollars, for comparability with Beach and Slotsve) generated from the microdata file. Also presented are the average income and the range of incomes for each decile. The reader will notice that there is no difference in the shares and only an insignificant difference between the average incomes calculated using the microdata file and those determined using interpolation of grouped data (Beach and Slotsve, Table 4). This result lends some support to the authors' methodology and, perhaps, to the use of interpolated grouped data when examining broad trends and patterns over time, as the authors do. However, more research is needed to examine the consistency of the differences between the two approaches.

It may be surprising to noneconomists that some Canadians have reported incomes of zero dollars or lower; indeed, in 1990, 43,393 households and 115,994 individuals were in this situation. (Parenthetically, none of these is among Canada's several thousand homeless because the survey includes only those respondents with a permanent residence at the time of the survey.) The average income of this group was – $7,038. Even more surprising is that 42 percent of the heads of these households were employed, 26 percent were homeowners (most of them mortgage free), and

---

1 Interpolation involves the selection of a single value from within a range that is representative of that range. For example, given a range of incomes from $20,000 to $25,000, the computer might select $22,500 as the value most representative of the range if we believe there to be a fairly even distribution of incomes within the range.

Table 2: *Family Incomes by Decile Shares, Canada, 1990*

Decile Number	Share	Average Income	Minimum Income	Maximum Income
			(1991 dollars)	
1 (bottom)	2.3	$12,546	– $100,170	$18,684
2	4.1	22,272	18,684	26,038
3	5.5	30,113	26,038	34,011
4	6.9	37,679	34,011	41,402
5	8.3	44,976	41,402	48,576
6	9.6	52,395	48,576	56,231
7	11.1	60,431	56,231	64,916
8	12.9	70,493	64,916	76,472
9	15.6	84,806	76,472	95,175
10 (top)	23.7	129,530	95,175	3,108,484

Source: Statistics Canada, Microdata File of Economic Families, 1990.

17 percent had university degrees (compared with 14 percent for the population in general). Those with negative incomes are invariably self-employed persons who have declared business losses against other income.[2] In the various reports on poverty and inequality, these households are classified as the poorest of the poor.

Beach and Slotsve's methodology allows them to construct a consistent set of measures for the 1972–92 period. The main measures they use are quintile and decile shares, Gini coefficients, two polarization indexes, and several measures to gauge middle-class shares.

Quintile and decile shares and the Gini coefficient are the most familiar tools in the measurement of economic inequality. Decile shares, displayed above in Table 2, tell us what share or

---

2 For example, in 1990, there were 521 families with total incomes of – $94,858 (– $100,170 in 1991 dollars). Each of these families contained a mortgage-free homeowner. They received only $1,100 in government transfers and paid about $6,400 in income tax.

percentage of total income each of the ten selected income group-ings receives. With quintile shares, only five income groupings are used. The Gini coefficient attempts to capture the degree of inequality in a single number between zero and one. The smaller the Gini, the greater the measured equality.

Polarization indexes are simply measures of the percentage of income flowing to recipients with either very high or very low incomes. For example, Beach and Slotsve define polarization index 1 as the share of all families with incomes above or below 0.5 of median income. Since median family income in 1991 was $46,742, Beach and Slotsve find that 40.7 percent of the popula-tion had incomes below $23,371 or above $70,113. Finally, middle-class shares are a complement to polarization indexes. One of the definitions of "middle class" that the authors use is the proportion of families with incomes *between* 0.5 and 1.5 of the median. Thus, in 1991, that share must have been 59.3 percent.

Results

Before presenting the evidence on income inequality, Beach and Slotsve reveal trends in average and median real family incomes. Starting in the 1960s, real family incomes have grown less quickly with each successive decade. This trend has been so sharp that real median Canadian family incomes grew a scant 0.3 per-cent per year, on average, from 1980 to 1989. This compares with 4.1 percent in the 1960s, and 3.1 percent in the 1970s. The turning point appears to have occurred around the mid-1970s.

Beach and Slotsve decline to explain this dramatic change, undoubtedly because their focus is on relative, rather than abso-lute, trends. However, such slow growth and the prospect of falling real incomes should be of great concern to all Canadians. One can point to structural economic change, poor fiscal manage-ment, rising payroll taxes, and, possibly, an increased climate of uncertainty as some of the (labor) demand-side factors. On the supply side, some of the demographic influences mentioned ear-lier, as well as the work-disincentive effects of certain social programs, may help to explain income stagnation. While it is the case that average family size has declined over the same period, thus serving to offset to some degree the slowing growth rate of incomes, the trend is clear: young families have little justification for rising expectations.

The major results of the study deal with distributional changes in family incomes and with middle-class shares. On the question of polarization of family incomes, Beach and Slotsve track both polarization indexes for the 1972–92 period. They also present two other measures of polarization: population shares and income shares. The former tell us the percentage of the population that is either below or above a certain cutoff value (such as 0.5 of the median), while the latter tells us the percentage share of total income received by families whose incomes are below or above that same cutoff income value.

Beach and Slotsve find that, while there is clear evidence of changing polarization in *individual* earnings over the period — up for men, down for women — there is no statistically significant trend in polarization of *family* incomes even after cyclical factors have been accounted for. This, they argue, results from income pooling within families, government transfers, and the offsetting effect of the male and female trends. This is a very important result because it contradicts a widely held view that incomes are becoming increasingly polarized in Canada. Anyone who has followed the discussion of social policy issues in recent years, especially in the popular press, will have been told repeatedly that income disparities are growing, that the rich in Canada are getting richer and the poor, poorer. This claim is made without a shred of supporting evidence, yet some journalists, commentators, and even academics continue to repeat this canard in the belief, perhaps, that it must be true since they have heard it so often. I hope, without much optimism, that these folks will look at the Beach and Slotsve study.

The second major result concerns the middle class. Because there is no widely accepted definition of "middle class," Beach and

Slotsve use a variety of measures, all of which are relative in character in the sense that they regard "middle class" as a position in the middle of the income distribution, rather than as a particular standard of living or as a concept of common interests. Specifically, they use five measures of population shares (such as between 0.5 and 1.5 of the median), five measures of income shares, and four additional (quintile) income shares (middle 20 percent, middle 40 percent, middle 60 percent, and middle 80 percent).

The evidence Beach and Slotsve present in their Table 14 mirrors, as one would expect, the polarization results: the overall decline in the share of income going to the middle class over the 1972–92 period has been modest. However, regression results indicate that cyclical factors are significant and that, once the cycle has been accounted for, there is no statistically significant trend in middle-class shares over the period. To borrow from Mark Twain, reports of the demise of the middle class have been greatly exaggerated.

The fact that economic recessions increase the degree of polarization should not be a surprise. When people become unemployed, their incomes usually fall dramatically. In 1990, for example, the average income of households in which the head was unemployed was only $32,500, compared with $51,100 for households in which the head was employed. This means that many more households, even some formerly high-income households, will find themselves in the bottom income groups. This results in an increase in measured polarization. With economic recovery, many of the unemployed get jobs, which moves them out of the bottom income groupings and, frequently, into the middle class.

Although Beach and Slotsve have undertaken an impressive and important study, they nevertheless can be criticized for their single-minded focus on income as an indicator of well-being. Income, as the authors are aware, is an imperfect measure of the actual standard of living a family enjoys. Such things as in-kind benefits — subsidized housing, in particular — do not show up in the official income statistics, nor do gifts and loans, which are important resources for low-income students. Mortgage-free home ownership — which reduces the household's required spending on housing and thereby improves the living standard over others at the same income — also does not show up. As well, certain types of income, such as social assistance and unemployment benefits, are significantly underreported, according to Statistics Canada. And there is, of course, the growing underground economy.

Household consumption, rather than income, may be a better choice of indicator for economic well-being. Consumption tells us directly about a household's standard of living, which is, after all, what we are chiefly interested in. Our expectation is that household consumption levels will show less inequality than household income levels. This is because, as economists have long suggested, people tend to borrow or save to smooth out transitory changes in income. Unless the changes in income are perceived to be permanent, people will try to maintain a relatively stable level of consumption. The lifecycle hypothesis illustrates this nicely. Young adults, who are, on average, much lower on the income scale than their parents, will often consume more than their income. Later, in their peak earning years, they typically will consume less than their income as they save for retirement. The theory predicts, among other things, that consumption will be far less volatile than income.

Evidence drawn from Statistics Canada's Family Expenditure Survey confirms this hypothesis. Table 3 shows average current consumption and average current consumption per capita by quintile for 1982, 1986, and 1992.

The top-to-bottom-quintile ratio is a handy measure of inequality. In terms of current consumption, the average top-quintile household consumed four times as much as the average bottom-quintile household in 1982. In terms of incomes, the top-to-bottom ratio in 1982 was approximately ten. While it is impossible to identify a trend from only three values, there is certainly no evidence here to suggest a rising rate of inequality of consumption

Table 3:   *Consumption Trends by Household*
           Income Quintile, Canada, 1982–92

Quintile/Year	Current Consumption			Current Consumption per Capita		
	1982	1986	1992	1982	1986	1992
Lowest	$8,460	$10,553	$14,442	$5,096	$6,596	$8,700
Second	14,759	18,296	23,178	6,099	7,920	10,077
Third	19,478	24,800	30,790	6,858	8,702	11,404
Fourth	24,752	31,920	38,789	7,640	9,791	12,635
Top	33,816	44,402	54,882	9,802	12,368	16,237
Ratio of top to bottom quintile	4.00	4.21	3.80	1.92	1.88	1.87

Source: Statistics Canada, *Family Expenditures in Canada*, cat. 62-555, various issues.

during the 1980s. More revealing is the second half of the table, which shows per capita household consumption (calculated by dividing average household current consumption into average household size) by quintile. These data tell us that, typically, consumption per person in the top quintile is only about twice that in the bottom quintile and that, in fact, the degree of inequality declined slightly over the past decade.

The data on Canadian consumption provide a somewhat different perspective in answering the question: Are we becoming two societies? These data point, I think, to an even more emphatic no! The use of consumption rather than income as an indicator of material well-being also casts some doubt on the conclusion that the United States is becoming two societies. Research by University of Texas economist Daniel Slesnick (1994) shows that inequality of consumption, once adjustments are made for family size and other factors, has declined by 23 percent since the end of World War II, and that there was no "U-turn" in inequality during the 1980s. Mayer and Jencks (1992) track the ratio of top-quintile consumption to that of the bottom quintile between 1973 and 1989 and find that it rose slightly from 4.78 to 4.81, while the comparable ratio for income increased much faster, from 7.95 to 9.79 over the same period. They conclude that "there was not an increase in inequality to make any fuss over."

"Middle class" is an eminently relative concept. Literally, it refers to some middle grouping in an entire distribution. Is there, however, an "absolute" element in what is commonly perceived as a middle-class lifestyle? Are there particular consumption goods, for example, that are now commonly associated with a middle-class standard of living? Is it possible that ownership of items such as a color television or an automobile bestow a sense of having arrived in the "middle class" or at least a sense of belonging to the mainstream? And if this is the case, can trends in the household ownership of these consumer durables reveal something about the fate of the middle class? The problem with this approach is that it cannot be applied to any particular individual or household and that it is by no means a timeless standard. Applied to large aggregates, however, such trends can be a useful indicator of the middle class.

Table 4 is an unsystematic and incomplete comparison along these lines. The four items listed are those middle-class durables for which consumption data exist since the mid-1970s. The table shows that ownership of some durable goods commonly linked to the middle class is increasing. In a real sense, more people are enjoying middle-class comforts now than was the case in the 1970s. It is interesting to note that, while the percentage of all households owning an automobile has declined somewhat over the period, the percentage of car-owning households in the bottom quintile has been fairly stable.

Policy Issues

I wish to take issue with several points that Beach and Slotsve make or imply in the area of policy. The first is their claim that government transfer payments are "inequality reducing." This is,

Table 4: *Household Consumption of
Selected Consumer Items, Canada, 1977–91*

	1977	1981	1985	1991
	(percent of households)			
All households				
Color television	72.4	84.9	93.3	97.5
Cable television	48.9	59.0	65.1	71.4
Dishwasher	23.7	33.1	38.1	44.2
Car	78.7	80.2	77.5	73.2
Lowest quintile				
Color television	54.5	70.6	84.5	94.5
Cable television	39.0	47.5	53.5	61.2
Dishwasher	7.6	11.2	14.7	17.9
Car	46.4	48.0	48.7	48.8

Source: Statistics Canada, *Household Facilities by Income and Other Characteristics*, cat. 13-218.

in fact, not clear: transfers have an indeterminate effect on inequality over time. While it is obvious that a redistribution of income from those above average to those below average will reduce the *current* level of inequality, that very redistribution process may serve to stifle both the current and future income growth of recipients. It does this in two ways.

First, on the supply side of the labor market, there is the disincentive to work inherent in most redistributive programs, as well as the long-term erosion of skills, confidence, and self-esteem that often accompanies dependency. On the demand side, there is the adverse effect of high taxes (to pay for the redistributive programs) on both consumers and firms. While income redistribution may benefit recipients in the short term, in terms of both income and leisure, it may well work to their long-term disadvantage. It may trap them at a lower level of income than would otherwise have been the case, leaving them with little hope of entering the mainstream of society. In short, redistributive policies may end up being "inequality *enhancing*." The point here is that we simply do not know how people's incomes would have changed in the absence of state redistribution of income.

Second, I wish to address the question Beach and Slotsve raise in Chapter 6: "Why should we be concerned about income polarization?" The authors argue that, if greater polarization is caused when people slip down the income distribution curve into privation due to economic forces over which they have no control, then this is a problem. Now, slipping down the distribution curve is one thing; deprivation and job loss are quite another. Poverty is a serious problem. Unemployment is a serious problem. But changes in the polarization and inequality measures that Beach and Slotsve use tell us nothing about either problem. By now, readers will be aware that people can slip down the income distribution curve simply by standing still. Indeed, their relative position can slip because their incomes are increasing more slowly than the average. Beach and Slotsve also imply that there is something intrinsically unfair about rising inequality. Again, it seems to me that we need to know the source of the change in inequality before we make any moral judgments.

The reader should also question Beach and Slotsve's recommendation that the state become more involved on the demand side of the economy as a means of reducing unemployment and, presumably, income polarization. Even a casual observer of government activities over the past two decades could argue that it has been precisely government policies that have reduced productivity and efficiency and contributed greatly to the slackness in the labor market. Poorly structured income support programs such as unemployment insurance and welfare have had a negative effect on the incentive to work. High taxes, regulatory excess, and bureaucracy have had a detrimental effect on risk taking and entrepreneurship. And Canada's public debt, now over $500 billion at the federal level, has pushed up real interest rates and exerted a negative effect on investment in capital. This is to say nothing of errors, waste, and mismanagement. Why should we expect the state to be any more successful in the future than it has been in the past, especially in a more complex, global economy?

In fact, a stronger case can be made for less, not more, government involvement. A dynamic economy with high labor productivity, innovation, and a sellers' market for workers may simply be inconsistent with a strong government presence in the economy. Higher economic growth and the creation of more and better jobs that all of us, including the authors, want for society may be incompatible with the kinds of income support programs we have in place now.

Beach and Slotsve have assembled a wealth of statistical data relevant to the issue of polarization and the fate of the middle class. The variety of measures used, which they handle with care and technical skill, add greatly to the credibility of the effort. This empirical study makes an important contribution to the ongoing debate on social policy. The finding that bears most emphasis is that the "facts" appear to contradict the conventional wisdom about the disappearing middle class in Canada.

References

Mayer, S.E. , and C. Jencks. 1992. "Recent Trends in Economic Inequality in the United States: Income vs. Expenditures vs. Material Well-Being," discussion paper. University of Chicago.

Slesnick, Daniel T. 1994. "Consumption, Needs and Inequality." *International Economic Review* 35

Statistics Canada. *Canada Yearbook*. Ottawa. Annual.

———. Cat. 62-555. *Family Expenditures in Canada*. Ottawa. Annual.

———. Cat. 13-218. *Household Facilities by Income and other Characteristics*. Ottawa. Annual.

———. 1990. *Microdata File of Economic Families*. Ottawa.

A Comment

Alan Harrison

Late in 1994, a newspaper article about income inequality appeared under the title "The rich get richer, the poor get pummelled" (Drohan 1994, D2). A casual glance might have left a reader believing that this headline described Canadian trends — though, to be fair, the article's subtitle was somewhat circumspect about the Canadian situation: "Income inequality is widening in Britain, the U.S., and, *to a lesser extent*, Canada" (my emphasis).

The article, by a journalist from the newspaper's European Bureau in London, actually focused on the United States and the United Kingdom. Very little mention was made of Canada, except to acknowledge that recent trends in this country do not parallel those in the United States or the United Kingdom. This assertion is indeed true: the level of inequality in Canada, as measured by the (admittedly inadequate) Gini coefficient, has stayed relatively stable. But figures for the United States and the United Kingdom show increases in inequality, and alarm bells in those countries are ringing. According to Richard Freeman, for example, rising wage inequality in the United States "is now recognized as one of the nation's major economic problems" (1994, 1).

Lest the relative trends encourage observers in Canada to become complacent, social commentators have begun expressing concern about increased polarization within the income distribution. By increased polarization is meant "a decline in middle class jobs" or "a vanishing middle class" (Levy and Murnane 1992, 1338, 1339): those in the distribution's center are moving to one or the other of its tails, getting richer or poorer in the process.

The concept of polarization has attracted attention only relatively recently, although it has become almost as fashionable a concept as globalization and deindustrialization, with both of which it is sometimes linked. This argument attributes the "disappearing middle class" (Wolfson 1994, 353) directly to the migration of semiskilled jobs to Third-World (for which, read cheap labor) economies.

Though everyone agrees that increased polarization refers to declines in the proportion of the population with "middle-class" incomes, there is less agreement on how to measure the degree of polarization. Broadly speaking, there are two approaches. Sometimes, the proportion of the population whose incomes lie within some specified range around the median income (the income that divides the population in half) is reported. If this proportion falls over time, this change is taken as evidence of greater income polarization. Alternatively, the range of incomes for a fixed population group is considered instead: the population's individuals are first ranked by income and, then divided into, say, quintiles (the top 20 percent, and so on); polarization is measured as the distance between the highest and lowest incomes for the middle 20 percent, divided by median income. In this case, an increase indicates greater polarization.

Different measures can, of course, lead to different results, but Wolfson argues, not unreasonably, that, if several different measures agree — that is, if all point to a change in the same direction — this typically indicates "an unambiguous change in polarization" (1994, 357).

This is the fray that Charles Beach and George Slotsve enter. To cut to the chase, before I briefly describe the buildup, they answer the question "are we becoming two societies?" with a resounding "no." They do not mean that nothing is happening, but rather that what is happening is explainable as a direct consequence of (among other things) business cycle fluctuations — in other words, it is not an inexorable trend, but a reversible phase.

Beach and Slotsve arrive at this conclusion after long and careful analysis of data for Canada from the past 20 years or so. They look first at information on individual earnings by sex and then at individual income, again by sex.[1] Next, they consider family incomes, arguing that income is a resource shared within the family. There follows an assessment of the impact of changes in tax burdens, accomplished by investigating polarization in post-tax family incomes. Last, they briefly examine whether family incomes are becoming more or less insecure. Along the way, Beach and Slotsve refer to a series of regression equations (the details of which are relegated to an appendix) that measure the role of cyclical factors in causing observed fluctuations in polarization.

It is important to note that increasing inequality and greater polarization do not necessarily go together. Wolfson points out, with characteristic bluntness, that equating polarization with increased inequality "entails a fundamental conceptual error" (1994, 353), and he provides a theoretical example as proof.

In general terms, the argument goes as follows. Inequality comparisons can be based unequivocally on Lorenz curves[2] only when these curves do not intersect. If one curve lies outside the other, the distribution that yields the curve further from the line of equality is unambiguously characterized by the greater degree of inequality. For a particular pair of distributions, Wolfson shows how one can exhibit an unambiguously greater degree of inequality, but a lower degree of polarization, than the other.

Wolfson goes further. Using a time series of Statistics Canada's Survey of Consumer Finances, he shows how, from 1973 to 1981, Lorenz-based inequality measures declined at the same time as there was evidence of increased polarization. Thus, Wolfson shows that "[t]he divergence between polarization and inequality is not merely a theoretical curiosity; it occurs in practice as well" (1994, 358).

---

1 Income is defined as earnings plus nonlabor income.
2 See Beach and Slotsve's appendix for an explanation of the concept of a Lorenz curve.

Beach and Slotsve's study of polarization is not, then, just another in a long line of studies of income inequality. It represents a new research direction. The authors begin by noting that polarization is "best thought of as a complement to inequality" (p. 54), and they do not focus on inequality measures.

Beach and Slotsve provide points on the Lorenz curve, but not in the conventional way, which is to supply the changing income share associated with a particular population share. (Thus, we might be told that the 20 percent of families with the highest incomes received 41 percent of total income in 1979 and 41.5 percent in 1987.) Instead, Beach and Slotsve use the median income, and multiples thereof, as reference points, measuring the proportion of the population between incomes on either side of the median. That is, they use the first of the two approaches described earlier.

For example, according to their Table 12, in 1972, 18.5 percent of families had incomes that were less than half the median income; their share of total income was 5.3 percent. The equivalent 1992 figures were 18.0 and 5.43 percent, respectively. Families with incomes above 1.5 times the median represented 20.1 percent of all families in 1972, with an income share of 39.1 percent of total incomes. By 1992, the equivalent figures were 23.1 and 43.8 percent, respectively. Those in the middle, then, represented 61.4 percent of all families and 55.6 percent of total income in 1972, but had declined to 58.9 percent of all families and 50.7 percent of total income in 1992 (Table 14).

The figures in the previous sentence typify the greater polarization Beach and Slotsve reveal. Even before any attempt is made to assess the contribution of business cycle fluctuations, the changes do not suggest the decimation of the middle class. In this context, Beach and Slotsve have done us a great service. The debate over polarization, like many others that relate to social policy, is often characterized by a great deal of heat but not a lot of light; this study yields enough light to cast a shadow over arguments that the middle class has gone the way of the dodo.

In short, the Beach and Slotsve contribution is a significant one. That said, however, economists can usually find something to criticize in other economists' research, and I am no exception in this regard. In what follows, I will suggest how this study could have proceeded differently.

The least satisfactory aspect of most such analyses may be their tendency to compare snapshots at different points in time. People's fortunes fluctuate. On reading that "the rich get richer [and] the poor get pummelled," some think that yesterday's rich are all richer today, and yesterday's poor are all suffering a more serious plight. Certainly this is true for many of yesterday's rich and poor, but the data behind this headline tell us only that today's rich people, whoever they are, are relatively richer than were yesterday's rich, whoever they were. (To be precise, the data do not even say this, since words like "rich" refer to stocks of wealth, while most of the data cited usually refer to income, which is a flow.) Most data are silent on whether today's and yesterday's rich (or poor) are the same people.

Imagine that each morning a lottery determined our income for that day. If we got a good draw in the lottery, we could save what we did not spend; if we got a bad draw, we could borrow. Next day, another lottery would determine our income afresh. Of course, life is not, like this, but if it were, we would still see inequality. Depending on the lottery's nature, we could also see variations in polarization through time. Yet we might reason that, because good and bad draws even out over the life cycle, inequality and polarization at any given time are not worth worrying about.

We might worry, though, about persistence. If yesterday's rich are today's rich, and yesterday's poor are today's poor, we might choose to devise policies designed to make the persistently poor a little better off at the expense of the persistently rich. How might we assess the degree of persistence? Ideally, we would use data on a panel of families that we could follow through time. Such panel data have not been readily available in Canada, and Beach and Slotsve recommend developing a set.

Nobody would take issue with the plea for panel data. By their nature, though, panel data do not quickly address the questions we would like to ask of them. In the meantime, another approach might approximate at least some of what we could learn if and when panel data become available.

If people expect to have good and bad draws, they build that expectation into their financial planning. A good draw typically leads to some saving, while a bad draw leads to some dissaving — or, for those without assets, to some borrowing. Thus, no one must give up eating because of one bad draw. In short, consumption (that is, current expenditure) smooths out to some degree the fluctuations introduced into the income stream by the lottery.

The reader might ask, What does this have to do with polarization? The answer is, a lot. Consider the situation where we have only snapshot (that is, no panel) data, but this information covers both income and expenditure. Such data are much more likely, on average, to give a reliable picture of an individual's or a family's long-term well-being. Put differently, consumption data typically represent more informative snapshots than do income data.

This contrast is particularly pertinent in the current context. Recall that Beach and Slotsve find that most of the increased polarization they observe can be attributed to business cycle fluctuations. This discovery suggests that, when the economy improves, there will be a concomitant reduction in polarization. On the other hand, they also find that family incomes became less secure between the mid-1970s and the mid-1980s.

These results point in obvious directions. A recession, in essence, is a time when a disproportionate number of people get bad draws in the lottery. If they expect an upturn in the economy, this might be reflected to some extent in their consumption behavior, which will smooth out the downturn (though this effect will admittedly be mitigated by their observation that many people are in the same boat as they are). If, however, their incomes really are more insecure, they may attempt to live within their current means and not make plans based on a brighter future. In short, consumption data could help us determine which of these findings is more important quantitatively.

Finally, let me ponder the question of what all this has to do with social policy. In this context, consider the evidence for the United States, where inequality and polarization have increased markedly over the past 20 years. Early in their study, Beach and Slotsve refer to the work of Blackburn and Bloom (1993), who suggest that the difference between the US and the Canadian experiences, at least where changes in inequality are concerned, can be traced in part to differences in the emphasis on social policy in the two countries.

Beach and Slotsve repeatedly echo this point, though in such a way that many might not fully appreciate it. Their conclusion, for example, implicitly contrasts the Canadian experience with the US one: they write that the 1980s were "not so much a new era of polarization in Canada as an era of slower economic growth, higher taxes, and two severe recessions that had marked distributional effects" (p. 126).

Significantly, social policy is not mentioned here, despite its role in mitigating the effects of "slower economic growth, higher taxes, and two severe recessions." More could have been made of this connection in a contribution to a series on social policy. Like Mark Twain (and, for the moment at least, Unitel), the welfare state could justifiably claim that reports of its death have been greatly exaggerated.

To conclude, it is appropriate to revive my earlier positive tone. Beach and Slotsve have carefully, and without the rhetorical flourishes that often characterize this issue, laid to rest the claims of the soothsayers of doom. For this, they deserve our heartfelt thanks.

References

Blackburn, McKinley, and David Bloom. 1993. "The Distribution of Family Income: Measuring and Explaining Changes in the 1980s for Canada and the United States." In David Card and Richard Freeman, eds., *Small Differences that Matter: Labor Markets and Income Maintenance in Canada and the United States*, National Bureau of Economic Research Comparative Labor Market Series. Chicago; London: University of Chicago Press.

Drohan, Madelaine. 1994. "The rich get richer, the poor get pummelled." *Globe and Mail* (Toronto). December 17.

Freeman, Richard B. 1994. "Program Report: Labor Studies." *NBER Reporter*. Fall.

Levy, Frank, and Richard Murnane. 1992. "US Earnings Levels and Earnings Inequality: A Review of Recent Trends and Proposed Explanations." *Journal of Economic Literature* 30. September.

Wolfson, Michael. 1994. "When Inequalities Diverge." *American Economic Review: Papers and Proceedings of the 106th Annual Meeting of the American Economic Association* 84. May.

The Contributors

Charles M. Beach is Professor of Economics at Queen's University in Kingston, Ontario, where he has taught since 1972. He obtained his Ph.D. from Princeton University. His principal areas of research are income distribution, empirical labor market analysis, and applied econometrics. He has published five books, including *Labour Market Polarization and Social Policy Reform* (edited, with Keith Banting, 1995), and numerous papers in labor economics and econometrics. He was a co-founder and secretary of the Canadian Econometrics Study Group, co-initiator of the Canadian Household Panel Survey initiative, a co-founding member of the Canadian Employment Research Forum, and chair of the Data Liberation Initiative. He has also been Editor of *Canadian Public Policy* since 1995.

Alan Harrison is Professor of Economics at McMaster University in Hamilton, Ontario. He worked for some years on income and wealth inequality and, more recently, he has turned his attention to outcomes of wage bargaining between unions and private sector firms. His publications include papers in the *American Economic Review*, the *Canadian Journal of Economics*, the *International Economic Review*, the *Journal of Labor Economics*, and the *Review of Economic Studies*.

Chris Sarlo is Associate Professor of Economics at Nipissing University in North Bay, Ontario. His research interests include poverty, inequality, and the role of the state. He is the author of *Poverty in Canada* (Fraser Institute, 1992).

George A. Slotsve is Assistant Professor of Economics at Vanderbilt University in Nashville, Tennessee. He obtained his Ph.D.

from the University of Wisconsin—Madison in 1989. His fields of interest are theoretical and applied labor economics, income distribution, industrial relations, and applied econometrics. He has published articles in numerous journals, including the *Bell Journal of Economics*, the *Canadian Journal of Economics*, *Economics Letters*, *Industrial and Labor Relations Review*, and the *Journal of Income Distribution*. He is the co-author (with Charles Beach and François Vaillancourt) of *Incomes of Canadians: A Study of Distributional Change* (Statistics Canada, forthcoming).

Members of the
C.D. Howe Institute*

* The views expressed in this publication are those of the authors and do not necessarily reflect the opinions of the Institute's members.

Sharwood and Company
Shell Canada Limited
Sherritt Inc.
Sidbec-Dosco (Ispat) Inc.
Sierra Systems Consultants Inc.
Southam Inc.
Spar Aerospace Limited
Speirs Consultants Inc.
Philip Spencer, Q.C.
The Standard Life Assurance Company
Sun Life Assurance Company of Canada
Suncor Inc.
Swiss Re Life Canada
TELUS Corporation
Laurent Thibault
Thornmark Corporation
3M Canada Inc.
The Toronto Dominion Bank
The Toronto Stock Exchange
Torstar Corporation

Tory Tory DesLauriers & Binnington
TransAlta Utilities Corporation
TransCanada PipeLines Limited
Trimac Limited
Trizec Corporation Ltd.
Robert J. Turner
Unilever Canada Limited
Urgel Bourgie Limitée
Vancouver Stock Exchange
VIA Rail Canada Inc.
J.H. Warren
West Fraser Timber Co. Ltd.
Westcoast Energy Inc.
Weston Forest Corporation
Alfred G. Wirth
M.K. Wong & Associates Ltd.
Fred R. Wright
Xerox Canada Inc.
Paul H. Ziff

Honorary Members

G. Arnold Hart
David Kirk

Paul H. Leman
J. Ross Tolmie, Q.C.